Jane Kurtz and YOU

Read! Write! Dream!

Jane Kurtz

Jane Kurtz and YOU

Jane Kurtz

The Author and YOU

Sharron L. McElmeel, Series Editor

LIBRARIES
UNLIMITED
A Member of the Greenwood Publishing Group

Westport, Connecticut · London

Library of Congress Cataloging-in-Publication Data

Kurtz, Jane.
   Jane Kurtz and you / Jane Kurtz.
      p. cm. — (The author and you)
   Includes bibliographical references and index.
   ISBN-13: 978-1-59158-295-3 (alk. paper)
   ISBN-10: 1-59158-295-4 (alk. paper)
   1. Kurtz, Jane—Juvenile literature. 2. Kurtz, Jane—Homes and
haunts—Ethiopia—Juvenile literature. 3. Authors, American—20th
century—Biography—Juvenile literature. 4. Children's literature—
Authorship—Juvenile literature. I. Title.
PS3561.U6885Z46 2007
813′.54—dc22   2006032407
[B]

British Library Cataloguing in Publication Data is available.

Library of Congress Catalog Card Number: 2006032407
ISBN-13: 978-1-59158-295-3

First published in 2007

Libraries Unlimited, 88 Post Road West, Westport, CT 06881
A Member of the Greenwood Publishing Group, Inc.
www.lu.com

Printed in the United States of America

The paper used in this book complies with the
Permanent Paper Standard issued by the National
Information Standards Organization (Z39.48–1984).

10 9 8 7 6 5 4 3 2 1

To the Ethiopia community, including my own family, that shaped me into a storyteller and writer. Thank you.

Contents

Series Foreword

Have you ever wanted to sit down and talk with the author of a beloved story? Have you ever wanted to find out more? Good authors are like good friends. They touch our hearts and minds. They make us wonder and want to learn.

When young readers become engaged with a story, they invariably ask questions.

- What comes first in Bob Barner's books, the words or the pictures? How does Bob Barner make his illustrations? Does he sing the songs he puts in his books?
- How long does it take Jim Aylesworth to write and retell his stories? Did he always know that he wanted to be a writer and poet?
- How does Jacqueline Briggs Martin find the inspiration for her stories? How does she research the facts for her stories?
- Does Mary Casanova love the out-of-doors as much as her characters do? Did the stories she wrote really happen? What parts of her books are true?
- Is Jane Kurtz Ethiopian? Why does she write about Ethiopia? If she is from Ethiopia how come she knows so much about the Oregon Trail and Johnny Appleseed?

As teachers and librarians, we know that the moment children begin asking questions, we are presented with a wonderful opportunity. In response, we may hold discussions or create learning activities. Yet answers to some questions are hard to come by. After all, our students and we cannot just sit down and talk with the authors we love and admire. But wouldn't it be great if we could?

Libraries Unlimited has developed *The Author and YOU* series to give you the next best thing to a real-life visit with your favorite children's authors and illustrators. In these books, you'll hear from authors and illustrators as they reflect on their work and explain to YOU, the reader, what they really had in mind. You'll find answers to some of the questions you and your students might have, and to some you never thought to ask.

Just as each author or illustrator is a unique individual, his or her conversations with YOU will be unique and individual. There is no formula, no pre-designed structure. We've simply asked each author or illustrator to discuss the things they think are important or interesting about themselves and their books—and to share their comments with YOU.

Some authors will provide actual ideas and plans for you to use in sharing books with young readers. Others will share inspirations that will help you generate your own ideas and connections to their work. In some cases, the author writes the book in collaboration with another. In others, it is a private reflection; but in all cases you'll discover some fascinating information, and come away with valuable insights.

Previously this series has featured some notable authors and illustrators: Gerald McDermott, Alma Flor Ada, Toni Buzzeo, Jim Aylesworth, Jacqueline Briggs Martin, Mary Casanova, and Bob Barner. This current addition to the series is written by Jane Kurtz, an author who creates her stories with words she has gathered as the wordsmith that she is. Kurtz uses rhymes and rhythms to entice readers into her picture books—and lyrical prose, well-developed characters, and interesting plots to bring readers into her novels. We are excited to present Jane Kurtz's perspective on her life and writing.

It is our hope that by giving you these special messages from authors and illustrators, *The Author and YOU* series will increase your joy and understanding of literature—and in turn, will help YOU motivate young readers, surround them with literacy and literacy activities, and share the joy of understanding.

Sharon Coatney
Sharron L. McElmeel

PART I

Readers and Writers

From Reader to Writer

I wouldn't be a published author today except for two things. The first is that I was born stubborn. The second is that I can't remember a time when I didn't love books.

This book lover didn't have a library. I was nine years old before I sat my fourth-grade self down on a concrete floor and looked up at the delicious sight of spines and titles lined up like rows of corn waiting for me to open them up and start reading.

Books were precious and rare because I grew up in a remote part of Ethiopia, a country in East Africa. My Ethiopian friends didn't have paper and pencils in their homes. Nobody in the village of Maji, Ethiopia, had even heard of a place where people could borrow books for free. The only school for miles around—a building with mud-and-straw walls on the outside and mud benches on the inside—had just six grades and no library.

When my parents moved to Ethiopia from the United States, they brought barrels full of things, including books, with them from America.

Jane learning to read

Maji, Ethiopia school building

A few shelves full of books sat like treasures in our living room. I read the same pages and chapters over and over, as hungry to visit the characters again as if they were beloved next-door neighbors. I loved books and words and stories.

Ethiopia was bursting with interesting words. One that sounded to me like *fwa-fwa-tay* means "waterfall." The young men and boys who spent hours working around our house and yard to earn money for pencils and paper and other things they needed for school taught my mother other words. One word they taught her sounded like *berah-beroh*, which means "butterfly." The day she learned the word she excitedly passed it on to my sisters and me. She said she thought the word, as it came out of people's mouths, sounded like the flapping wings of a butterfly.

The countryside around Maji was also bursting with stories. No one, including me, had television or movies to watch or radios to listen to, so people took time to sing stories, dance stories, and tell stories. My sisters and I made up stories and acted them out for days at a time.

Does that mean I wanted to be an author when I grew up? No. I didn't know any authors. No published author ever came to visit my school, and I never saw any until I was in college. My sisters and I did play a card game called "Authors." The authors on those cards wore lace collars and had long beards. I looked at the pictures and thought all authors must have died a long time ago.

My mom was the one who taught us all how to read. Luckily for me, she adored books. Even though she hadn't yet finished college at that time, she was an enthusiastic reader, and everyone around her knew it. My dad read, too. Reading helped him learn how to put a small machine called a "ram" by one of the waterfalls so it would pump water up to our house so the donkeys wouldn't have to carry it anymore.

One of our parents read aloud to us almost every night. Before bedtime, my sisters Cathy and Joy would get to climb onto Dad's lap—because they were the youngest—and my oldest sister, Carolyn, and I would lean against each of his arms, and he would finish reading a chapter.

"So when did you get to be an author?" people ask.

When I was young, people often told me that I was a good writer. In fact, my second-grade teacher wrote on my report card, "Jane has been a joy to work with. We have enjoyed her poems. They are exceptionally good for her age. Perhaps it is one of her talents."

During high school, a story I wrote for an English class was published, and I was both proud and embarrassed. In college, I sent some poems to literary magazines, and a few of them were accepted for publication. By this time I was taking all the creative writing classes I possibly could and got used to people telling me I was a good writer.

After I graduated from college, I decided I wanted to write short stories, but since I knew little about the craft of writing, I received a lot of rejection letters—hundreds and probably thousands of rejection letters.

But I was determined to learn. I read magazine articles about the craft of writing. I bought books and checked books out of the library about writing. Most important of all, I practiced. I wrote and wrote and read and read and wrote some more.

When I started to have my own children I discovered just how many children's books I didn't know existed. Week after week, I took David, Jonathan, and Rebekah to the Carnegie Public Library in Trinidad, Colorado, where we were living, and we brought home armloads of books.

My children sat on my lap, and—just as my parents had done—I read aloud to them every day. Every evening I read chapters from my favorite books or from new books we discovered together. As the children grew older and we went on trips, I read to them in the car to make the miles and hours slip by. I read books from the series The Chronicles of Prydain by Lloyd Alexander and *The Watsons Go to Birmingham—1963* by Christopher Paul Curtis. Long books. The boys loved dragons and castles, so I tackled the *Lord of the Rings* trilogy, skipping a few of the more detailed descriptions. Rebekah, who was too

Jane reading to her sons

young to follow the plot, still liked the poem about troll bones and asked me to read it again and again.

All of that reading has helped me become a writer. At the time I'm writing these words, I've had twenty-three books published. But when I first started to write books for children and send them to publishers, I got a whole new giant stack of rejection letters.

But since I am stubborn, I persisted and kept learning about the craft of writing. I've put some of what I have learned in this book in hopes that it will help you, too.

A Writer's Job

When skillful readers pick up a piece of paper, read the words they find written on it, and say, "Wow, this is good," they often don't take the time to analyze what, exactly, they mean by "good." But many teachers and editors have tried to understand what makes writing good. Are there certain traits in writing that inspire or delight or amuse avid readers?

The answer is yes.

It takes practice to spot these traits in other people's writing and in your own. But as you develop this skill, you are doing one of the most important parts of a writer's job. In the following chapters, I'll show you examples to help you understand these traits.

IDEAS

Good writers gather ideas that are interesting, focused, and based on things the writer knows about and cares about.

A writer's job is to have interesting ideas. If you decide to write about "home, sweet home," you'll have a hard time getting the reader to sit up and pay attention because the reader has run into that idea before. Readers are quick to yawn and put something down if they think, *I already know that*. In this book, I'll show you examples of how writers get fresh ideas from three places: memories, observations, and research.

VIVID DETAILS

Good writers are treasure hunters for vivid, interesting details that will pull the reader inside the experience or inside the writer's thoughts.

A writer's job is to be a detective, always hunting for vivid, fascinating details. One important secret of good writing is that sometimes you can write about an old, stale idea, and if your details are wonderful, they make the reader think about the old notion in a new way. You can even write about "home, sweet home," if your details are good enough. Ironically, writers mostly get vivid details from three places: memories, observations, and research.

WORD CHOICE

Good writers use words that are specific and interesting, words with sparkle and pizzazz.

A writer's job is to collect, polish, and play with all kinds of words. Funny words. Unusual words. Intriguing words. Some words soothe. Others seem to punch the reader right in the stomach. Words can be as specific and direct as nails sliding right into a piece of wood. Sparkling words grab attention and often create a picture in the reader's mind.

RHYTHM AND BEAT

Good writers listen to the rhythms of sentences and pay attention to how one sentence flows into and fits with the next.

A writer's job is to develop a good ear for pleasing patterns of words, sentences, and paragraphs. (Reading aloud is a big help when it comes to this trait.) In the same way you may drum your fingers along with a song, a good story or expository page has a rhythm and a beat. The sentences and paragraphs flow gracefully and smoothly into each other.

PERSONALITY AND VOICE

Good writers know that a piece of writing—like a person— has a personality.

A voice that is bland and boring or annoying or garbled will make readers turn away. An entertaining or confident voice invites the reader in. The writer's job is to find the right voice for each piece of writing. Sometimes—when a carpenter is reading an instruction manual, for instance—the only important thing is that the voice be clear and calm. But other kinds of voices are fun to play with and give readers pleasure. Sassy voices. Funny voices. The kind of voice that comes from stringing words together in ways that make a reader want to weep. The type that forces us to pay close attention and is even frustrating, perhaps, but rewards us at the end with the feeling of, *Whoa, that was worth the work.* Just as people can be entertaining and compelling to listen to when they talk, people can be entertaining and compelling to listen to when they write.

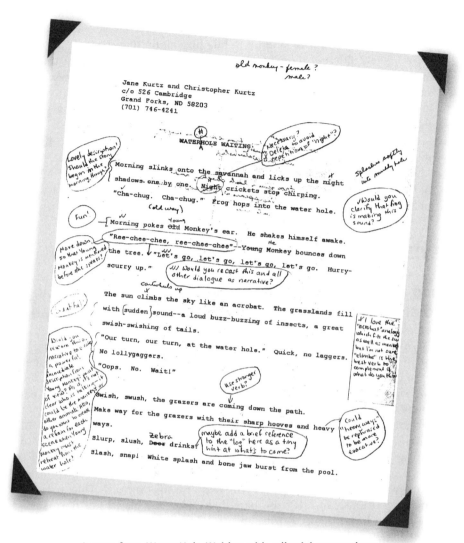

A page from *Water Hole Waiting* with editorial suggestions

ORGANIZATION

Good writers organize, working hard to find the best structure for a piece and a compelling beginning, middle, and end.

A writer's job is to know that readers don't want to flounder around in the middle of a confusing, mucky swamp of words. Readers get impatient if they have to find their own path through the mire. In fact, readers even become irritated if a writer hasn't already done the job of Getting Things Organized.

- Sometimes, getting the path figured out is only a matter of taking a little bit of time and writing more than one draft. The challenge is that when people talk, their minds often go chugging along like this: one thought … a completely different thought … an entirely, completely different thought … an absolutely, entirely, completely different thought. Some people write the same way. It takes practice to write a thought and back it up with one detail and another detail and perhaps an example or two before going on to the next thought.

- Sometimes, getting the path figured out is complicated and hard and makes writers want to run screaming into the night. That's when it's particularly helpful to study different strategies other writers have used. It often helps to make a collection of how other writers solved their organizational puzzles.

REVISING IDEAS AND CONVENTIONS

Good writers revise bravely and boldly, making big changes, and also revise patiently and carefully, making tiny changes.

Writers need to become good readers of their own work, because a writer's job is to rewrite. Most writers aren't that pleased by what they come up with on the first try. A first draft is like a pile of clay that the writer had to work really hard to dig up. While I'm wiping the sweat away and leaning on my shovel, exhausted from all that digging, I groan a little bit, knowing I have another hard job ahead—that of shaping the clay into a beautiful pot. Digging is tough. Having to throw away some of the clay I dug up is even tougher. Trying to get a decent-looking pot into shape is so tough that sometimes I give up at that stage. But putting on the final, polishing touches? That part, to me, is gloriously fun. It's the part that makes me glad I was born stubborn and loved books, words, and stories enough to want to become a published author.

PART II

The Bookshelf

BICYCLE MADNESS

Bicycle Madness. Reading Level: Ages 7–11. 122 pages. Henry Holt and Company, 2003.

Frances Willard, a central character in my short novel, was a real American social reformer who lived in the 1890s. It was an interesting challenge to weave into the story her real words, her real house, and her real bicycle. I made up Lillie, who is terrified of a spelling bee but who gathers courage from her next-door neighbor's determination to ride a bicycle in the days when women wore skirts to their ankles and weren't allowed to vote.

Book cover illustrated by Beth Peck from *Bicycle Madness.*
Illustrations © 2003 by Beth Peck. Reprinted by permission of Henry Holt and Company, LLC.

About the illustrator

The editor of *Bicycle Madness* asked Beth Peck to illustrate the book because of Peck's reputation for doing careful historical research. Indeed, she did a great deal of research, contacting the Frances Willard House in Evanston, Illinois, with a number of questions that would help her get the details right.

DO KANGAROOS WEAR SEAT BELTS?

Do Kangaroos Wear Seat Belts? Illustrated by Jane Manning. Reading Level: Preschool and Up. Unp. 32 pages. Dutton Children's Books, 2005.

A boy visits the zoo with his mother, sparking a series of questions about how animals stay safe. Do monkeys have to wear helmets? Do penguins ride in strollers? Does a young hippo have to hold *his* mother's hand? I used rhyme for both the boy's questions and the mother's playful answers as a way of creating a fun read-aloud story about a serious subject.

Book cover art by Jane Manning from *Do Kangaroos Wear Seat Belts?* © 2005 by Jane Manning. Reprinted by permission of Dutton Children's Books.

About the illustrator

Jane Manning has had the joy of illustrating a book that was on the *New York Times* best-seller list, and I looked forward to seeing what her funny, whimsical art would do to my story for this picture book. One of her challenges was how to use color to show the difference between the times when the narrator is imagining things—a penguin in a stroller, a bush baby in a backpack, and so on—and the times when he and his mom are looking at real animals in the zoo.

FARAWAY HOME

Faraway Home. Illustrated by E.B. Lewis. Reading Level: Ages 6–10. Unp. 32 pages. Harcourt, Inc., 2000.

After I came to the United States for college and in the following years, I struggled to talk about Ethiopia, and when my own children came along, I realized they were growing up far from my childhood home. Those emotions and experiences shaped *Faraway Home*, a story of Desta— a girl who considers America home—and her father, who is homesick for Ethiopia. The memories the father shares are, in reality, mostly my memories, including the flock of pink flamingoes rising against the pale sky.

Illustrations from *Faraway Home* by Jane Kurtz.
Illustrations copyright © 2000 by E.B. Lewis.
Reprinted by permission of Harcourt, Inc.

About the illustrator

When E.B. Lewis was in Ethiopia working on *Only a Pigeon,* he and my brother, Christopher, traveled outside the city of Addis Ababa to the beautiful town of Dembi Dollo. It was the home of an excellent school for rural students, where E.B. Lewis held an art class. Later, his photographs of rural Ethiopia helped him create the scenes for *Faraway Home.* He used a letter sent to my father from Ethiopia for the spot illustration on the front pages.

THE FEVERBIRD'S CLAW

The Feverbird's Claw. Reading Level: Ages 10–16. 295 pages. Greenwillow/ HarperCollins Publishers, 2004.

A girl who lives protected in a walled city is kidnapped by a roving band and struggles to get home—only to find that she now understands secrets at the heart of the city. When I set out to create a world with three different civilizations in an uneasy relationship with each other, I was inspired by my background in reading fantasy books and by my complex memories of Ethiopia. I also used my knowledge of and research into how different cities and societies worked in the days before they had writing, money, or many of the things we take for granted. It took thirteen years to work out all the details of this world.

Cover art copyright © 2004 by Don Seegmiller. Used by permission of HarperCollins Publishers.

FIRE ON THE MOUNTAIN

Fire on the Mountain. Illustrated by E.B. Lewis. Reading Level: Ages 4–10. 40 pages. Simon & Schuster, 1994.

In this retelling of an Ethiopian folktale I heard as a child, I made the main character into a dreamer who survives the test of a night on a cold mountain. He then uses his sister's help to outwit the rich man who would cheat him out of his victory.

Reprinted with the permission of Simon & Schuster Books for Young Readers, an imprint of Simon & Schuster Children's Publishing Division from *Fire on the Mountain* by Jane Kurtz, illustrated by E.B. Lewis. Illustrations copyright © 1994 by E.B. Lewis.

About the illustrator

This was the first children's book illustrated by E.B. Lewis. After he created the watercolors for this book, he went on to illustrate many others, including three with a Coretta Scott King Honor Award for his illustrations, and another that was named a Caldecott Honor Book. His work has been called "arrestingly beautiful."

I'M SORRY, ALMIRA ANN

I'm Sorry, Almira Ann. Illustrated by Susan Havice. Reading Level: Ages 7–10. 120 pages. Henry Holt and Company, 1999.

School Library Journal called my short novel for young readers "a perfect title for exploring pioneer life." A deep friendship between two girls who were born on the same day ends up strained by their hard lives traveling in covered wagons on the Oregon Trail. Sarah, with her hasty spirit, accidentally hurts her friend Almira Ann and has to find a way to say "I'm sorry."

Book cover and interior art illustrated by Susan Havice
from *I'm Sorry, Almira Ann.* Illustrations
© 1999 by Susan Havice. Reprinted by permission
of Henry Holt and Company, LLC.

About the illustrator

Susan Havice's goals for the black-and-white illustrations in each chapter of the book were that they would interest young readers and also that the details would be "exactly right." As each illustration was drawn she put it up on her wall. She writes, "I could look back and forward to see that Sarah was the same from beginning to end. This growing string of illustrations put Jane Kurtz's story right in front of me. Clothes had to be the kind people might have worn as they traveled west. Wagons had to be just like the ones that were pulled by the family's heavy, strong oxen. Even Queen Victoria, Almira Ann's doll, needed to look just right."

IN THE SMALL, SMALL NIGHT

In the Small, Small Night. Illustrated by Rachel Isadora. Reading Level: Ages 5–10. Unp. 32 pages. Greenwillow/HarperCollins Publishers, 2005.

Kofi and and his big sister, Abena, are awake at night, thinking about both the people and the stories they've left behind in Ghana, and also about the new situations and challenges that lie ahead in America. The stories Abena remembers and tells her little brother about tricky Ananzi and his sons, Vulture, Turtle, and Eagle, give them both courage. The *Washington Post* named this book one of the five best picture books of 2005.

Illustrations copyright © 2005 by Rachel Isadora. Used by permission of HarperCollins Publishers.

About the illustrator

Rachel Isadora's illustrations have won the prestigious Caldecott Honor Award and have brought her many fans because of her ability to draw readers close for a look at her characters. She lives in New York City and chose the city's skyline for the background in several of the book's illustrations.

JOHNNY APPLESEED

Johnny Appleseed. Illustrated by Mary Haverfield. Reading Level: Ages 5–7. 32 pages. Aladdin Paperbacks/Simon & Schuster, 2004.

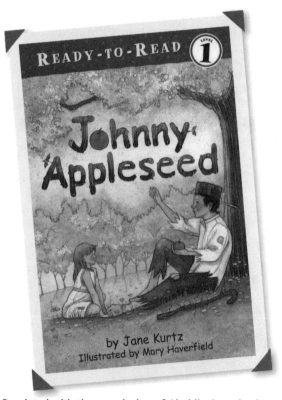

John Chapman, who came to be widely known as "Johnny Appleseed," has been made into a folk legend and a tall-tale character in some stories, but his real life was actually amazing. Other excellent books provide the facts of Johnny Appleseed's life, so I focused on creating a fun read-aloud book to celebrate his generosity and love of both apples and people.

Reprinted with the permission of Aladdin Paperbacks, an imprint of Simon & Schuster Children's Publishing Division from *Johnny Appleseed* by Jane Kurtz, illustrated by Mary Haverfield. Illustrations copyright © 2004 by Mary Haverfield.

About the illustrator

Since a lot has been written (and drawn) about Johnny Appleseed, Mary Haverfield wanted to start by learning everything "current and not so current" about her subject. She needed to know what kind of clothes he might have worn. She looked at farm buildings and houses of the time and studied apple trees in all seasons. When she was ready to draw, she based her Johnny Appleseed on a man who once worked for her husband. The model for the blonde girl was his daughter.

JAKARTA MISSING

Jakarta Missing. Reading Level: Ages 10–16. 268 pages. Greenwillow/HarperCollins Publishers, 2001.

Two sisters who have been living overseas learn about living for one year in a small town in North Dakota. In some ways, Dakar—the viewpoint character in my most autobiographical novel—is more like me than any of my other characters. She loves the sounds of words and stories. She has been to boarding school. And she adores her older sister, Jakarta. (Unlike myself and my sisters, the girls were named after the cities in which they were born.) In other ways, Dakar is based on my daughter, who was in middle school in North Dakota at the time I was writing this book.

Used by permission of HarperCollins Publishers.

MEMORIES OF SUN: STORIES OF AFRICA AND AMERICA

Memories of Sun: Stories of Africa and America. Edited by Jane Kurtz. Reading Level: Ages 10–17. 263 pages. Greenwillow/HarperCollins Publishers, 2004.

Africans living in Africa and the United States and Americans who are living or have lived in Africa responded to my request for short stories about the lives of teenagers in Africa today. Funny and sad, poignant and hopeful, fifteen stories and poems give a glimpse into how life is lived in East, West, South, and North Africa, and also into what it's like to move between cultures and countries.

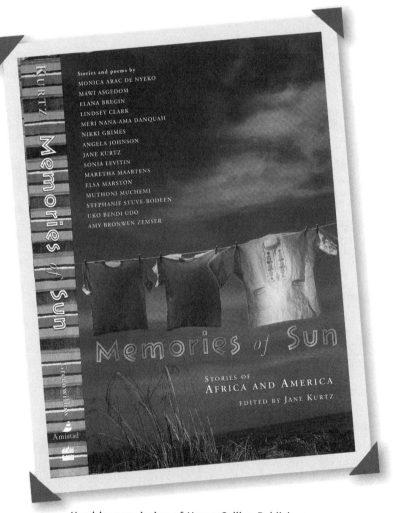

Used by permission of HarperCollins Publishers.

MISTER BONES: DINOSAUR HUNTER

Mister Bones: Dinosaur Hunter. Illustrated by Mary Haverfield. Reading Level: Ages 5–7. 32 pages. Aladdin Paperbacks/Simon & Schuster, 2004.

For this ready-to-read book, I wanted to give readers a peek at some of the things that fascinated me about the dinosaur hunter who discovered the first Tyrannosaurus Rex fossil. For example, Barnum Brown wore ties and fancy hats while he poked through the dirt in Montana, and people said it was as if he could smell bones. I also wanted to use lively language. It was a fun puzzle to see if I could juggle syllables, facts, and words.

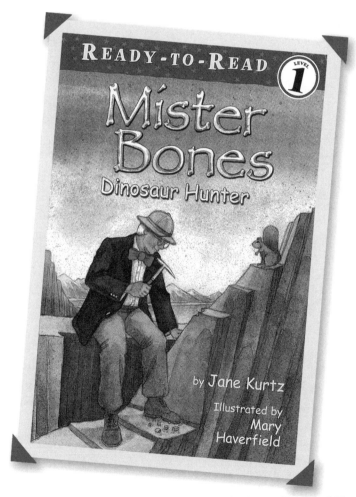

Reprinted with the permission of Aladdin Paperbacks, an imprint of Simon & Schuster Children's Publishing Division from *Mister Bones: Dinosaur Hunter* by Jane Kurtz, illustrated by Mary Haverfield. Illustrations copyright © 2004 by Mary Haverfield.

About the illustrator

Like me, Mary Haverfield wanted to learn about the real Barnum Brown and was determined to pin down details, such as what kind of hat he wore. Once her sketches were approved by the art director and editor, she got out her watercolor paints and started adding layer after layer. After the color felt right, she used a brown pencil to emphasize certain lines and added highlights with white gouache—water-based opaque paint she uses to add color and correct mistakes. She calls it "handy stuff!"

ONLY A PIGEON

Only a Pigeon. Co-authored by Christopher Kurtz. Illustrated by E.B. Lewis. Reading Level: Ages 6–10. Unp. 32 pages. Simon & Schuster, 1997.

This picture book tells the true story of Andualem, a boy who used to shine my brother's shoes. Andualem taught my brother to raise pigeons and gave him a glimpse into a hard life, but one in which children still find ways to be hopeful and kind. While my brother and I were writing this book, he taught me about pigeons, and I shared with him some of the important things I'd learned about writing and publishing.

Reprinted with the permission of Simon & Schuster Books for Young Readers, an imprint of Simon & Schuster Children's Publishing Division from *Only a Pigeon* by Jane Kurtz, illustrated by E.B. Lewis. Illustrations copyright © 1997 by E.B. Lewis.

About the illustrator

Christopher Kurtz and E.B. Lewis paid their own way to travel to Ethiopia for the art research on this book. By that time, the real Andualem, the boy whose story we told in *Only a Pigeon*, was too old to be a model, but he led them to younger boys raising pigeons in Addis Ababa. E.B. Lewis took pictures of boys, pigeon coops, and the city of Addis Ababa to use in his watercolor paintings.

PULLING THE LION'S TAIL

Pulling the Lion's Tail. Translated into Amharic by Yohannes Gebregeorgis. Illustrated by Eshetu Tiruneh. Reading Level: Ages 6–10. 32 pages. Ethiopian Children's Book and Educational Foundation, 2006.

In my retelling of another beloved folktale from when I was young, when Almaz's father tells her he will be remarrying, she is impatient for love. "Much of what is good comes slowly," her grandfather warns, but she is sad and frustrated—until he sends her to pull hair from a lion's tail. This book was originally published in the United States by Simon & Schuster with illustrations by Floyd Cooper (1995, op). In 2006, the book was translated into Amharic, and published with both English and Amharic text.

Book cover for *Pulling the Lion's Tail* by Jane Kurtz, created by Eshetu Tiruneh © 2006 by ECBEF. Reprinted with permission of Ethiopian Children's Book and Educational Foundation.

About the illustrator

Eshetu Tiruneh, an Ethiopian artist, created watercolor illustrations for the 2006 Amharic edition of *Pulling the Lion's Tail.* In contrast to Floyd Cooper's oil paintings (for Simon & Schuster edition), Tiruneh's illustrations seem lighter and more naïve, and representative of the emerging children's book publishing efforts in Ethiopia.

RAIN ROMP: STOMPING AWAY A GROUCHY DAY

Rain Romp: Stomping Away a Grouchy Day. Illustrated by Dyanna Wolcott. Reading Level: PreK and Up. Unp. 32 pages. Greenwillow/Harper-Collins Publishers, 2002.

My daughter, who never missed a chance to splash in water and hated to quit, gave me a real-life model for the narrator, who also refuses to quit—arguing that the sky, the wind, and the rain agree with her. After she rushes outside in bad weather, her parents join her for a rousing stomp that turns into a romp and ends in a warm hug by the fire and the assurance that, grouchy or not, we are loved.

Illustrations copyright © 2002 by Dyanna Wolcott. Used by permission of HarperCollins Publishers.

About the illustrator

Dyanna Wolcott has illustrated many books with glorious watercolors in bright splashes of color. She lives with her husband and daughter in a small seaport town in the Pacific Northwest—a place where sometimes the rain falls for 90 days out of 120 and where gray skies can bring grouchy feelings to children *and* adults.

RIVER FRIENDLY, RIVER WILD

River Friendly, River Wild. Illustrated by Neil Brennan. Ages 6–10. Unp. 40 pages. Simon & Schuster, 2000.

Waters rise. A family leaves without their cat (assuming they will be gone only a few days). An entire city evacuates. Six weeks of fire and flooding later, they return to rebuild their lives. These poems that tell my city's real-life story won the Golden Kite Award for best picture-book text from the Society of Children's Book Writers and Illustrators.

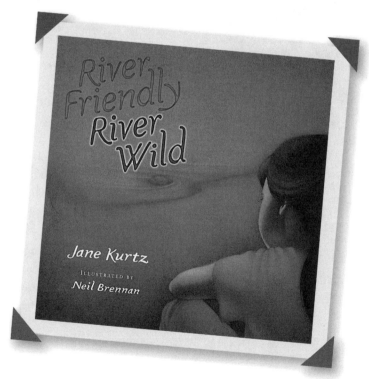

Reprinted with the permission of Simon & Schuster Books for Young Readers, an imprint of Simon & Schuster Children's Publishing Division from *River Friendly, River Wild* by Jane Kurtz, illustrated by Neil Brennan. Illustrations copyright © 2000 by Neil Brennan.

About the illustrator

I sent Neil Brennan many, many newspaper reports and photographs that I had taken in the city of Grand Forks after the floodwaters receded and we were able to return. He used my papers, drying on the lawn, in one painting. Kiwi in the book looks nothing like my real cat, however. The editor told me she chose this illustrator in order to contrast his "cool" style with the "heat" and intensity of the poems.

SABA: UNDER THE HYENA'S FOOT

Saba: Under the Hyena's Foot. Reading Level: Ages 8–12. 207 pages. American Girl, 2003.

Saba has been living with her grandparents in a remote part of northern Ethiopia. Now Grandfather has died, and Saba is fearful upon hearing strange sounds in the forest near where she collects water. When she and her brother are seized and carried off to the castles of Gondar, Saba is the only one who can unlock the mystery. What's her history? What happened to her parents? And where has her brother been taken? A student told me, "I like *Saba* because my favorite books are mysteries, and I liked to put the clues together."

Saba: Under the Hyena's Foot—Book cover art reprinted with permission of Pleasant Company Publications/American Girl. *Saba* is available through www.ethiopiareads.org and proceeds support literacy efforts in Ethiopia.

THE STORYTELLER'S BEADS

The Storyteller's Beads. Reading Level: Ages 10–14. 154 pages. Harcourt, 1998.

One reviewer called my first novel an "exquisitely crafted, sparely told tale of courage and friendship." Sahay, a young Ethiopian girl fleeing war and hunger, is thrown together with Rahel, who is from the Beta Israel (Jewish) community. Though the girls have been raised to mistrust and fear each other, survival in a refugee camp and an airlift to Israel opens their eyes—and hearts.

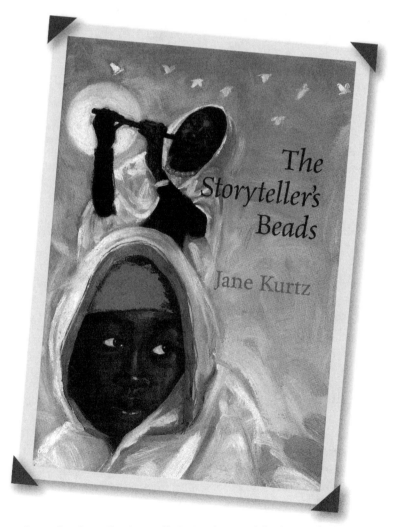

Illustration from *The Storyteller's Beads*, copyright © 1998 by James Ransome. Reproduced by permission of Harcourt, Inc.

TROUBLE

Illustration from *Trouble* by Jane Kurtz. Illustrations copyright ©
1997 by Durga Bernhard. Reprinted by permission of Harcourt, Inc.

Trouble. Illustrated by Durga Bernhard. Reading Level: Ages 4–8.
Unp. 32 pages. Harcourt, 1997.

Trouble always finds Tekleh. His father gives him a *gebeta* (an African game often called mancala) board, saying that a gebeta board always keeps a young boy out of trouble. The next day, Tekleh wanders from one trouble to the next, making trades, and ends up with a gebeta game and his father's praise. I set the folktale from my childhood in the country of Eritrea, once part of Ethiopia.

About the illustrator

Durga Bernhard listened to Eritrean drumming, kept *injera* (Ethiopian bread) batter fermenting in her kitchen for three days, and ate a meal wrapped in a *netela* (cotton shawl) that I loaned her, so that her mind's eye would find the colors she needed. She went jogging and jumped over ditches. Then she was ready to create a mischievous boy. In a touch that was a fun surprise (in fact, the editor had to point it out to me), in her cover illustration, Tekleh's stick is bumping the "u" out of place.

WATER HOLE WAITING

Water Hole Waiting. Co-authored by Christopher Kurtz. Illustrated by Lee Christiansen. Reading Level: Preschool and Up. Unp. 32 pages. Greenwillow/HarperCollins Publishers, 2002.

Morning slinks onto the savanna, and a thirsty young monkey keeps making dashes to the water hole while his mother tries hard to keep him out of the way of other animals. My brother and I used words and phrases, including similes and metaphors, to capture the ways animals look and sound as they approach water holes in the grasslands of Ethiopia, Kenya, and other African countries.

Art copyright © 2002 by Lee Christiansen. Used by permission of HarperCollins Publishers.

About the illustrator

Christopher and I had an e-mail conversation with a researcher who studies vervet monkeys in their natural habitat, and our editor asked her if she would be willing to also review Lee Christiansen's illustrations. When the monkey expert told him that monkeys don't smile when they are excited (their mouths make an "o" shape), Lee changed his pencil sketch for the cover.

Ethiopia: Books, Words, and Stories— *Fire on the Mountain* and *Pulling the Lion's Tail*

When my parents decided to move to Ethiopia, Carolyn was four, Joy was one, and I was the two-year-old squeezed in between them. I have vague memories and a pocketful of family stories about that trip.

The five of us walked up the plank onto a ship called the USS *America* and found the room where we would sleep as we crossed the ocean. It had two bunks, a double bed, a porthole, and a big bouquet of flowers that friends had sent. Then we all trooped onto the deck to wave to the Statue of Liberty as the ocean liner slid out into the Atlantic Ocean.

For eight days, Joy, Daddy, and I ran up and down the hallways of the ship, while Mom tried to read. She and Carolyn were seasick. Whenever a siren blew for a safety drill, Mom and Dad had to get us girls, grab life jackets, and rush to our assigned station. In calmer moments, Daddy took Joy and me swimming in the ship's pool and finally coaxed Mom and Carolyn into trying it, telling them it was good for seasickness.

For Carolyn, swimming didn't help. She was grumpy to the last—even through the captain's

Jane in the middle

end-of-trip party, scowling under her party hat. She was grumpy as the ship sailed into port at Southampton, England. She was grumpy as she walked down the gangplank early in the morning in her little blue coat. A man at the bottom called up to her, "Come on now, Nora. Let's not look like that." Carolyn didn't smile.

By then, Daddy wasn't smiling, either. When the ship doctor had given us our final shots, he'd carelessly emptied an entire syringe of typhoid medication into Dad's arm. Now that we were in England, Dad struggled to carry Joy, the car bed, and all of our suitcases into the train station at Southampton. When he finally stood at the ticket window, rubbing his swollen, sore arm, he discovered the train was delayed.

My tired mom slumped on a bench. Daddy gathered Carolyn, Joy, and me, all of us wearing our heavy coats, around him and began to tell us a story. "This is the house that Jack built. This is the malt that . . ." Even when things were falling apart, he was a great storyteller.

From the train we boarded a plane. When we landed in Rome and again in Athens, we climbed off the plane briefly. It was cold even in our winter coats. After more hours and hours of flying, we came out of the clouds and began to descend toward Cairo, Egypt. Carolyn looked out the righthand side of the plane at the Mediterranean Sea, lapping on the shores of Alexandria. She pointed to the lights on the bay and said, "It looks like a string of beads."

By now, Mom and Dad had become experts at getting us into our boots, coats, and snowsuits. We stepped off the airplane into a blasting heat that sizzled up from the ground and ran up under our clothes and turned our faces boiled red and sweaty. As soon as we got inside the terminal, Mom began stripping and peeling our warm clothing away.

Ethiopian Airlines flew only twice a week. In the shade of a pyramid, my mom watched my dad climb onto a camel and galump off into the desert. She wondered if she'd ever see him again—and was relieved to see the camel eventually lumber back.

When the morning of our departure came, my parents woke us up at about 3:00 A.M. and herded us aboard an airport bus that hurtled through the streets of Cairo. From the way the driver drove, it seemed to my parents that the bus had a gas pedal and a horn but no brakes. After we'd waited at the airport for hours and hours, someone came to tell my father that the airplane had mechanical difficulties.

We tried again the next morning. This time, the twin-engine plane roared into the sky, landing after a little while to refuel at Port Sudan. "Talk about hot!" my mom said to my dad. The five of us sat, wilted, in the terminal. Apparently, I was "a trooper." My mom later told me, "You didn't have any choice." She added that not many children traveled in the early 1950s, and everywhere we went, the attendants took good care of us.

LEARNING A NEW LANGUAGE

For two years, we lived in a house in Addis Ababa, where Ethiopian teachers came to our home and sat for hours listening to my parents as they practiced speaking, reading, and writing Amharic words.

Over the vast continent of Africa, Ethiopia was the one country that developed its own alphabet still in use today. Each time we walked by the nearby girls' school, we heard students chanting out Amharic letters as the teacher pointed to a chart. Every letter family on the chart had seven letters. The chanting sounded like this: Beh, bu, bee, bah, bay, BIH, boh. Seh, su, see, sah, say, SIH, soh. And so on through every one of the thirty-three families.

Fwa-fwa-tay and *berah-beroh* are written this way in Amharic:

ለቡረ ቆ
ኳ ኳ ቴ

One day when I was three, it started to rain, and I ran inside, shouting, "It's zin-ah-bing."

Three-year-olds don't understand "this is the language of English" and "this is the language of Amharic." They just like to repeat words.

When I was four, we moved to Maji. Now, my world was full of round things. Our new house was round, like most of the other

houses around Maji. The walls were made of adobe mud, baked hard in the sun. The roof was made of a special kind of grass. The house wore its roof like a hat pulled down low. A round clay top sat at the tip.

I lived in a compound with a fence made out of thorny trees spreading their arms in a big circle around the outside. Inside was a grassy circular road lined with cedar trees. The trees whooshed and whispered in the wind and waved their branches at the buildings—a house for us, a house for the teacher, a house for the nurse, a clinic for the sick and injured, a storage building, and a workshop where the Jeep was always being repaired. (The school was so big that it didn't fit inside the compound, but sat just outside.)

GROWING UP IN MAJI

Whenever I speak to adults or children, they have some of the same questions.

Who did you play with?

Ethiopian friends came to the round compound to play with my sisters and me, and we sometimes went to their houses.

By the time Ethiopian children are about seven years old, they have important jobs. Girls help make food. Boys are often sent out to tend the family sheep or goats. When my sisters and I got to be that age, we mostly played with each other, making up elaborate stories that we acted out. On the hillsides around Maji, we often saw the boys watching sheep, goats, or cows.

What did you eat?

My mom grew up in little towns in Iowa, so when we moved to Maji, she brought recipes for roast beef, mashed potatoes, Jell-O, lemon meringue pie, and other things her mom used to make. So we ate lots of those. When we had visitors from England, they looked at the Jell-O and roast beef together on their plates and asked, "Why do you mix sweet and savory?"

My dad's parents were homesteaders and farmers in the sagebrush hills of eastern Oregon. When we moved to Maji, he took seeds for a big garden like the one his mom used to tend. So we ate lots of vegetables. Ethiopian friends frowned at the salads on their plates and asked, "Why do you eat things the goats eat?"

My mom became a cooking teacher to the boys and young men who were earning money for school supplies, and our kitchen was often crowded. As she worked beside them and showed them how to boil drinking water or separate egg whites for meringue, she tried to get them to speak to her in Amharic so she could learn new words, while they tried to get her to speak to them in English so they could learn new words.

Plenty of things needed to be done in the kitchen—heating water, pushing pieces of wood into the tiny door on the stove that cooked our food, kneading dough for loaves of bread, and chopping vegetables. Sometimes, one of the young men killed a chicken out in the backyard. I sat in a tree and watched. The chickens flapped around the yard even after their heads were cut off. Bits of blood and feathers flew.

Eating with friends

That chicken might get fried up and drumsticks passed around. Other times, chickens went into *wat*, a stew that was spicy and red. We didn't have to use forks when we ate *wat*. It was made to be scooped up with *injera*, sour and spongy. *Wat* and *injera* was what my Ethiopian friends ate every day. They chewed chunks of sugar cane and spit the white fiber onto the ground. So did we. Their houses were full of the smell of roasting coffee beans, and ours was too.

Were you hot all the time in Africa?

Actually, most of the time, I was chilly. Fog rolled through the valleys, filling them up, and sometimes was so thick on the mountaintop that my sisters seemed to disappear. My mom reminded us to take our sweaters when we went outside to play. We always saw Ethiopian adults and children wearing what we called *shammas*, which is actually the name of the type of light cotton cloth the big shawls are made from.

Did you speak Amharic or English?

In Maji, my Ethiopian friends and I spoke Amharic together when pretending to make *wat* out of mud and *injera* out of leaves. After my

Woman holding *injera*

Ethiopian friends started working hard in their own houses, I was stuck around a lot of adults. While I heard them speaking Amharic, they did not turn to me and say, "And what do you think, little girl?" So I didn't get much practice saying Amharic words.

Ethiopia has seventy-nine other languages besides the language of Amharic that my parents were always trying to learn better. If I met a woman on the path, the way she greeted me might sound like this: "*Tin-est-te-ling.*" (That was the Amharic word for "hello.") But she might say "*Sah-ro.*" Or "*Jay-sha.*" She might not speak or understand Amharic at all, in which case, if my mom or dad wanted to talk to her, they would use a translator. My sisters and I thought the sounds of words were interesting—even when we didn't know what they meant—so we asked the schoolboys to teach us how to count to five in Deeze, their language. It sounded like a song when people were speaking it.

WORDS AND STORIES, STORIES AND WORDS

My sisters and I made up our own stories and acted them out, sometimes inside the house—cutting paper people out of catalogs and

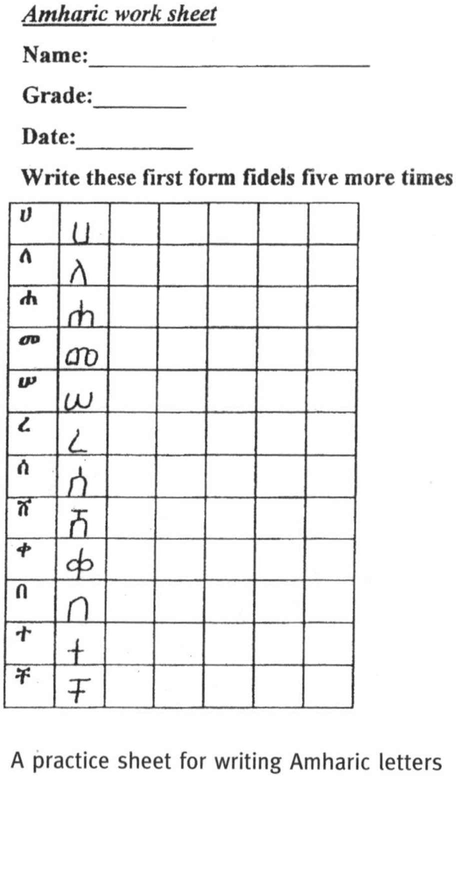

Amharic work sheet

Name:_____

Grade:_____

Date:_____

Write these first form fidels five more times

ሀ	ሀ					
ለ	ለ					
ሐ	ሐ					
መ	መ					
ሠ	ሠ					
ረ	ረ					
ሰ	ሰ					
ሸ	ሸ					
ቀ	ቀ					
በ	በ					
ተ	ተ					
ቸ	ቸ					

A practice sheet for writing Amharic letters

hanging them from cobwebs in the attic on rainy days, for example. But most of the time we were outside, climbing in the hills or running up and down the path that led to one of the nearby waterfalls.

When my dad took us on a trip out to the countryside and it was time to stop for the night, I would curl up in my sleeping bag and fall asleep to the sounds of the mule drivers telling stories around the fire and laughing as if they were having the party of the world. My dad could laugh as loud as anyone, and he was my favorite storyteller of all.

Once a week, my parents heated water in a huge kettle on the wood stove. When it was steaming hot, they poured it into the white bathtub and opened the tap to add the cold water that the ram pumped up from the river. Then all four of us girls (by now there were four of us) got into the bathtub at the same time, trying not to bash each other with our elbows and knees.

My mom would put shampoo in our hair and rub our heads with her strong fingers until she was sure our hair was clean. I always hated that part because my scalp was tender. But I kept quiet because I wanted to hear the story that my dad was reading aloud from his stool in the corner.

The path to the waterfall

After we were done with our baths, we ran to the stove in the living room to warm by the fire. We took turns as Daddy rubbed a towel briskly over our heads, making us giggle and forcing our hair to stick out every which way. Sometimes he pulled out the hair-cutting scissors and tried to even out our bangs. I wiggled so much that I sometimes ended up with a crooked line.

It's fitting that the first two-book contract I signed with a publisher was for two Ethiopian folktales from my childhood, *Fire on the Mountain* and *Pulling the Lion's Tail.* For ten years I had been knocking on a door that was locked. The key turned out to be something that had been dancing in my brain since I was two years old: Ethiopian words and stories. Stories and words.

Jane *(second girl from the right)*

WRITERS THINK ABOUT WRITING

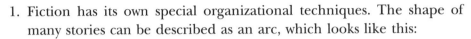

Organization
  Good writers organize, working hard to find the best structure and a compelling beginning, middle, and end.

1. Fiction has its own special organizational techniques. The shape of many stories can be described as an arc, which looks like this:

The arc usually begins with a main character who wants or needs something or has a problem that desperately must be solved. Usually, the character tries to get what he or she needs—or fix what's wrong—but fails again and again. If you've managed to make the reader care about your main character, your reader will feel more and more tense. That part of the story is called the "rising action." Make a list of all the things Almaz in *Pulling the Lion's Tail* does to get close to her new mother. Put them on the story arc, like this:

Eventually, a story reaches an important "this is it!" scene. Now the main character really must succeed ... or learn something from the experience of failure. Almaz's "this is it!" scene happens when she brings the lion's hair to her new stepmother. That scene goes at the top of the arc where the "x" is.

  Try making a story arc for a piece of fiction that you are working on.
2. The little tail at the end of the story arc is where the author often shows how something or someone (the main character) has changed from the beginning of the story to the end. In contemporary fiction, characters usually grow and change as they make their journeys. In folk literature, often it is only the outside circumstances that change while the person remains the same. In the story of Cinderella, for example, her circumstances change but she stays the same person she was at the beginning. Cinderella starts off sweet and poor (and unlucky). By the end, she is sweet and rich (and lucky).

  Use a chart similar to this one to compare *Fire on the Mountain* and *Pulling the Lion's Tail*. Which one is more like a traditional folktale and which more like contemporary fiction?

	at the beginning of the story	at the end of the story
Almaz's main character trait		
Almaz's circumstances		
Alemayu's main character trait		
Alemayu's circumstances		

Details

Good writers are treasure hunters for vivid, interesting details that will pull the reader inside the experience or inside the writer's thoughts.

I didn't have to agonize over the plots of *Pulling the Lion's Tail* and *Fire on the Mountain* because I was retelling stories I'd heard as a child. I did fill both stories with vivid details that came from my memories of living in Maji. Here are some of the things I experienced in my childhood that made their way into those books. Each is associated in my mind with one or more of the five senses.

- *Wat* and *injera* (taste and smell)
- Girls working inside their homes (sight)
- Boys watching animals out on the hillsides (sight)
- Fog (touch)
- Houses with grass roofs and mud walls (smell and touch)
- Amharic words (sound)
- Waterfalls (sound and touch)
- *Shamma* cloaks and shawls (touch and sight)

Choose a memory of a place you love or an experience that's vivid to you. Make a list of five sense details associated with that memory, details you might use in your writing someday. Discuss the memory with someone else—perhaps someone who has had some of the same experiences or someone who will ask you helpful questions—and see if you can expand your list.

Revising Ideas and Conventions

Good writers revise bravely and boldly, making big changes, and also revise patiently and carefully, making tiny changes.

Nobody finds the best ideas or words on the first try. When I tried to write a poem about my childhood love of words, you can see how many changes I made before I came up with this version:

When I was five
I became a poet.
My new home dripped with words,
luscious as papayas.
"Jaysha," people on the path said,
dipping their head hello.
"Jaysha," my sisters and I replied,
running to the bat cave,
the beard tree,
Red Rock,
and *nifas birr,* gate of the wind.
Spangled words dangled everywhere.
Some were ripe.
Some tantalized and teased, just out of reach.
I, the poet, couldn't wait to catch them.
"Dear Grandma," I wrote
in sprawling, scrawling letters.
"How are you? I am fine."

Troublemaker: The Story Behind *Trouble*

Every week, my mom sat at the dining room table and tap-tapped on her typewriter. She was writing letters to her mother back in Iowa and to my dad's parents in Oregon. Those letters recorded lots of ups and downs with me. Not long after we arrived in Addis Ababa, she wrote, "Janie is still a character and the Dennis the Menace of the family, though she's becoming a bit more dignified now at the advanced age of three."

The next mention of me was even more hopeful. "Janie is growing up and blossoming out in lots of ways, is in general becoming a sunnier little girl, though she still has her moments of being our Calamity Jane."

But soon Mom had to admit I was as outspoken as ever. "We went to the Russells for dinner Sunday," she wrote, "and as we were taking off our coats, Janie said, 'We didn't come here just to sit and talk.'"

The Russells had come to Ethiopia so long ago that the spring wagon they brought with them had the first wheels many Ethiopians had ever seen. Daisy Russell's children were all grown up, and she wanted to have a tea party just for us girls. When it was over, Daisy Russell was full of praise for my older sister. She told my mom, "Carolyn was born a lady."

Probably my mother hoped that if she gave me enough time, I might turn into a lady, too. One week she wrote, "Janie is in a brand new stage of seeming so much more grown up. She is so serious about everything, trying to learn to make letters, to color nicely. Everything all business with her now though still a spark of mischief flashes from her eyes now and then and she loves to play jokes."

Eventually, she decided I wasn't going to make it. "Janie is still Janie," a later letter says. "She still talks as much at the table somewhat to Mrs. Russell's disapproval but we can't seem to squelch her no matter what."

PETS AND WILD ANIMALS

For an active, wiggly person who loved the outdoors, Ethiopia's animals were endlessly interesting to me. Sometimes I am asked if I had a pet cheetah or lion. During my childhood, cheetahs, lions, elephants, giraffes, zebras, antelopes, and wildebeests galloped, sped, and lumbered over Ethiopia's grassy savannas. (However, Maji was 8,000 feet above the savanna.) Hippos and crocodiles bubbled in Ethiopia's warm, slow rivers and lakes. (Maji had cold, fast rivers.) Camels carried the belongings of nomads in the dry, sandy north. (Maji was green and full of fog.)

Wild boars lived in Maji, but I never saw one—only the tunnels they made in the thick brush. Village boys or drivers herded most of the animals around me, including cows, sheep, goats, donkeys, and mules. When crops were ripe, the boys took turns sitting on small platforms and throwing rocks to keep the monkeys away.

There was one dangerous animal I saw a lot. When we first arrived in Addis Ababa, Joy and I had our first clashes with army ants. In the

A *gebeta* game carved into a rock

middle of studying their Amharic lessons, my parents would hear wild screaming. When they ran outside, they would find me running from the big black ants with their ferocious pinching. Joy would just stand still and scream until someone pulled off all her clothes, even her diapers, and hastily brushed and pulled away every last ant.

After we moved to Maji, it didn't take long to find army ants there, too, carving little black streams through the grass, sometimes getting close to the places where people had carved out holes for outdoor *gebeta* games. My sisters and I crouched, watching with scared fascination. Stray ants that wandered away from the marching column bit our rubber sandals so hard that their heads stuck in the rubber even after their bodies dropped off.

One night when we were camping, Daddy woke up to hear a soft clicking sound on the canvas tent. He turned over in his sleeping bag, thinking he was hearing the patter of rain. Suddenly, something dropped on his head. Instantly, he knew it wasn't rain at all but ants climbing up the outside of the tent and starting to drop down inside. We had a wild scramble that night and couldn't go back to sleep until Daddy had dug a trench all the way around the tent and put poisonous powder in it.

Anyone would probably think it wouldn't be too hard to learn to stay far away from the thick black lines of ants, marching relentlessly forward, little rivers of fierce creatures. But it was always so fascinating to poke a stick into those rivers. At first, a little hump formed as the ants piled over the stick, not caring if they stepped on each other. Before I knew it, ants would climb up the stick and bite my fingers or sneak up under my pants and bite me on the legs. Just as I had done when I was three years old, I would run shrieking into the house.

Maybe because I was a little wild myself, I longed to tame one of the animals around Maji. I never gave up trying to coax the cats that roamed the compound catching mice into wanting to sit still long enough to be petted. I also came up with schemes to toilet train frogs and make mud houses for lizards. Even the little bugs we called "roly polies" were a possibility.

It's no wonder that when a man came to our door with a baby dik-dik, the smallest member of the antelope family, I put up "such a clamor," as my mother wrote, that she reluctantly gave in. Cathy went around proudly saying, "We call him Bambi and he's an envelope." My parents worried we couldn't keep the little animal alive—and we couldn't. Daddy dug a grave, and—for months— my sisters and I put flowers on it and cried.

Our pet dik-dik

We didn't have much better luck with a vervet monkey someone brought to our door. As much as I talked to it and tried to stroke its fur through the cage, it only bared its little teeth and tried to bite my fingers. Finally, it escaped and bounded off into the tallest tree by my favorite swing.

To the day we left Maji, I never gave up hope that someday I would have a pet.

TRYING TO DO BETTER

My parents didn't give up easily, either. When I look at pictures of me, I remember how many times my mom tried curling my hair and coaxing me into dresses.

When I was young, Ethiopian girls mostly wore clothes made from white cotton woven from thread that their mothers and grandmothers and aunts spun—pulling the cloud of cotton with one hand and turning a spindle with the other. Full spindles were taken to one of the men who wove cloth. Then tailors turned the cloth into white dresses

with bright borders. But the outfit wasn't finished without a matching *netela*, a shawl made from soft, fine *shemma* cloth woven from cotton.

Sometimes, my sisters and I got Ethiopian dresses for our birthdays or Christmas. Other times—since Maji didn't have any stores—my dresses came from the same place my books came from: the storeroom. It was full of boxes and barrels, and though I didn't realize it, my mom and dad had filled those containers full of clothes and shoes of various sizes. At Christmas or birthdays, new clothes or shoes mysteriously appeared.

More often, my mom or dad looked at Carolyn when she came to the breakfast table and said, "You know, I think that dress is getting too small for you." Guess who got the dress then.

Me.

Not surprisingly, I had a childhood full of scoldings. In fact, in Maji people took seriously that African proverb *It takes a village to raise a child,* so lots of people scolded me. Ethiopian adults would slap my hand and make me drop frogs and lecture me when I tried to catch lizards, because they believed those animals cause diseases.

Clothes from the barrel and Ethiopia

Luckily, books helped. I imagined myself as Jo in *Little Women,* so flawed and rough in comparison to her older sister, Meg. *The Little House in the Big Woods* was a book I never got tired of reading because Laura's parents so obviously loved her even though she wasn't as sweet and responsible as her older sister, Mary. And when I discovered Janie Moffat, who even had my name, I was ecstatic.

In *The Middle Moffat,* Mama always introduced Sylvie, who was sweet sixteen, as her oldest child. The family often said, "Let Rufus do it first because he is the youngest." Joey was the oldest son and had important jobs such as locking the doors and closing the shutters at night. "But when Mama introduced Jane, she just said, 'This is Jane.'"

THE MIDDLE MOFFAT

The Middle Moffat by Eleanor Estes (Harcourt, 1942, and renewed in 1970) p. 3.

Finally! Jane-the-middle-Moffat knew how I felt.

Sometimes my reading led to embarrassing moments, too. The first time I ever read the word *bedraggled* I had to admit it sounded a bit like me. I did try to take care of my things and my clothes, but unfortunately for Joy, who was next in line for my hand-me-down dresses, I didn't manage very well. I climbed trees in them. I stepped on the hems and the ties. I dripped *wat* on them. By the time they were too small for me, they sometimes looked bedraggled.

One night, I was wailing because I had left my stuffed dog, Queenie, outside. I was so upset my dad had to go out in the dark with a flashlight until he found and rescued her. "She's all wet," he said. "You can't take her to bed with you tonight."

"I love her," I told him. "Even if she is bed-raggled."

My parents laughed and laughed. When my mom explained that the word was "be-draggled," I was mad. That way sounded *wrong*, and the other way was perfect.

Luckily for me, beneath the scoldings and frownings was a lot of love. My parents might get exasperated, but they were also proud of what they called our "spunk," and admired the way we scrambled up mountain paths.

One of my sweetest memories is of sitting on Daddy's lap on the men's side of the church (women sat on the other side), listening to the Ethiopian preacher and trying to understand the Amharic words. When my father got up to say the benediction at the end, he would hand me to whoever was sitting next to him, and I would drowsily listen to Daddy's voice as he said the words of blessing and comfort.

Slowly, I did learn to be more polite and less demanding. But I never did learn to be a lady.

WRITERS THINK ABOUT WRITING

Ideas

Good writers gather ideas that are interesting, focused, and based on things the writer knows about and cares about.

My picture book *Trouble* uses a story I had heard as a child, but the main character was a man, not a boy. Some of the things he traded with were dangerous—a spear, for example. When I wanted to make this story *mine*, I had to decide what my main character's personality was like (and how to show that). You know why this sentence popped into my head: "Trouble always found Tekleh."

Notice the way I follow up my first sentence with three specific ways Tekleh tends to get into trouble. (One comes from my experiences and the other two from my observation.) Put your own name in the first sentence and follow up with three sentences from your experiences or observations.

Organization

Good writers organize, working hard to find the best structure for a piece and a compelling beginning, middle, and end.

Sometimes the best organization for a story is a circle. A story begins at one point and ultimately ends up back in the same place. That's the case with *Trouble*. While Tekleh spends the day caring for his goats, he makes trades for a knife, a musical instrument, a drum, a bag of corn, and a papaya. He ends up with another gebeta board.

1) Make a map of Tekleh's day—The circular aspect of the tale can be shown visually by creating illustrations in a circular pattern. In this way you can clearly see the circular nature of the story.

   Another way to create a picture of the story is to get a very long piece of white or brown Kraft® paper and cut it in a strip eighteen inches high. Then cut the strip into panels. Use each panel to create an illustration for one of the major events in the book. Finally, tape the illustrations together and tape the beginning to the end—so the story can start over again.

2) Expository writing often makes use of this type of organization. One of the most obvious places to look for models and examples is in magazines. Often the introduction to a story will be echoed in a clever way in the ending. Look at articles in children's magazines such as *Highlights* and *Cricket* to see if the writer ties the ending to the beginning.

Word Choice

Good writers use words that are specific and interesting, words with sparkle and pizzazz.

1) When I was thinking about how to draw the reader inside Tekleh's world, I considered the animals of my childhood. Make a list of the animals that show up in *Trouble*. How many of them were part of my real childhood?

2) Make a list of specific, interesting, unusual words to describe your own pet or your favorite animal. Use my writing as a mentor text. What words did I use to describe the camels? What words did I use to describe the dik-dik?

What words can you use to describe how the animal looks when it's moving or lying down, how it sounds, how its fur would (or does) feel? Challenge yourself to think of words no one else in the room will think of.

More circular stories

Bear, John B. *Frog and the Princess and the Prince and the Mole.* Tricycle Press, 1994.

Benjamin, Alan. *Buck.* HarperCollins Publishers, 1993.

Glaser, Omri. *Round the Garden.* Harry N. Abrams, 2000.

Hassett, John. *Mouse in the House.* Houghton Mifflin/Walter Lorraine Books, 2004.

Hogrogian, Nonny. *One Fine Day.* Simon & Schuster Children's Publishing, 1971.

Johnston, Tony. *Big Red Apple.* Cartwheel, 1999.

McGuire, Richard. *Night Becomes Day.* Puffin Books, 1997.

Murphy, Mary. *How Kind!* Candlewick, 2002.

Root, Phyllis. *Old Red Rocking Chair.* Arcade Publishing, 1992.

Schindel, John. *What's For Lunch?* HarperCollins Publishers, 1994.

Wilson, Sarah. *Loves and Kisses.* Candlewick, 1999.

Ziefert, Harriet. *I Swapped My Dog.* Houghton Mifflin/Walter Lorraine Books, 1998.

Ziefert, Harriet. *Oh, What a Noisy Farm!* Sterling, 1995.

Grandparents and Traveling "Home": The Story Behind *I'm Sorry, Almira Ann*

As my mother typed, I liked perching beside her with my pencil pressing hard against the knuckle of my "tall man" finger, so that I could carefully form words on a piece of lined paper. My letter would go beside hers in the envelope.

If I was lucky, I got to lick the stamp with its picture of His Imperial Majesty Haile Selassie. I knew all the mail would go into a big bag to be lugged by a mule down the mountain, where the Ethiopian Airlines airplane (the same one I flew on to Maji) would carry it to Addis Ababa and then halfway around the world.

It made me proud to be doing such a grown-up thing. One of those letters is my earliest saved piece of writing.

But my grandparents didn't feel real to me, even though I liked writing letters to them. Grandparents were something to be read about in books—not much more real than red shoes that danced by themselves or mermaids that turned to sea foam.

That changed when I was five. Grandpa and Grandma Kurtz took a break from their farm in Oregon and came to visit us in Ethiopia.

The night they arrived, Mom made a welcome-to-Maji supper. My sisters and I picked flowers for the table and made nametags to show where everyone was supposed to sit. "Your grandpa came here to help build us a new house," Daddy announced after we were all finally sitting down.

I peeked at my grandmother, who seemed stern. She'd grown up as a girl who was always expected to behave, even when her older brother teased her.

As an adult, she had raised five sons and one daughter on a dry farm during the Great Depression in the United States. She'd lived in one house where snow blew in through the cracks and homesteaded in another that was basically only a basement. For the next few years, her youngest child, Joyce, could not see outside unless she stood on a box or a chair.

Accidents with horses and guns killed her father and badly hurt two of her boys. All of her five sons went off to serve in World War II (and came back with sad memories).

She had to be tough to survive. But that night in Maji, I didn't yet know those things. "What did Grandma come for?" I asked.

Everyone laughed. "Just to be Grandma," my dad said. "Isn't that enough reason?"

WHAT GRANDMAS DO

Pretty soon I found out some of the things grandmas did. Mine took a lot of pictures with her Kodak camera. She said she wanted to show our cousins back in the United States how we played games based on the things we saw around us—such as the way people carried wood they needed for cooking. She talked about these cousins and about our aunts and uncles, asking, "Do you remember?" I had to say no. The only people we called "aunt" were the teacher who supervised the school in Maji and the nurse who ran the clinic.

Grandma started an embroidery class. I was proud to be included—until I saw that I had sewed my embroidery to the knee of my pants. Carolyn laughed as she used Grandma's little scissors to snip the threads.

"I can do it," I insisted.

In the second class, I sewed my embroidery to one of my socks.

At teatime that afternoon, Grandma told Aunt Marge and Aunt Ruth that Carolyn was a fine helper and was going to sew beautifully. She said Joy was the prettiest little girl she could ever remember seeing. Cathy was learning new words every day.

Jane *(on the left)* looking determined

I tried not to wiggle or slurp my tea. Surely she would say something about me next. "Janie ..." She paused. "Well, do I dare say that she is the *boy* of the family?"

Heads went nod-nod-nodding in agreement.

"Always out catching butterflies and frogs," Grandma said. "She surely shows her determined spirit."

I wished I could do something to make my stern grandma proud.

WHAT GRANDPAS DO: A NEW HOUSE

While Grandma ran her sewing classes, Grandpa and Daddy had meetings with the Ethiopian men who were going to show them how to build our new house. My sisters and I watched the workmen stomp around in a pit, mixing straw into the muddy clay. Then the wooden poles were set carefully into the ground in straight lines, because our new house wouldn't be round. And its roof was going to be made of corrugated tin, not grass. The floor would be cement. Goodbye to a mat over packed-down earth.

The new house would have something else the old one didn't have. Windows. When I saw Grandpa making window sills, I told him, "Now I can have a place to put my jars of frogs."

Finally one day, my mom was proud to show us that the living room was all plastered. "Isn't it smooth and nice looking?" she asked.

We ran our fingers along the straight, sleek walls. Not just anybody could do this kind of work. The man who was the expert knew how to knead exactly the right amount of straw in with the mud and clay to make the final coats in all the rooms. If he didn't do his job well, the walls would crack.

Then it was time for the floors. Workmen hauled a load of rock to the compound, enough for one room. Four men sat and broke the rock into little pieces—making a huge clanging noise. At supper, Daddy told us Grandpa had decided it was possible to make a cement mixer with part of an old truck and some other pieces lying around in the work building. "Really?" Mom asked, sounding skeptical.

But when the cement mixer was finished, it worked fine, even though Grandpa had a big blister on his palm by the end of the first day. Grandma took a picture with her Kodak camera of the first wheelbarrow full of cement. She often liked to say, "Never let a special time go by without taking a picture."

My dad liked to say, "Never spoil a special time by taking a picture."

After the house was finished, Grandpa and Grandma had to leave. Grandma's last sewing project was making hobo costumes for us girls by sewing patches onto our pants. During the Depression, she'd seen many of the men (nicknamed "hobos") who traveled around—gathering food as they could—trying to survive the hard times. She put cookies in bandanas and tied the little bundles to sticks. Out came the camera. Smile. Click. Even though we didn't really understand the idea of hobos, we trooped down to the garden, ate our cookies, and thought it was a grand party.

When the sad day came, we stood together and watched the Jeep with Grandpa and Grandma in it make its way up the hill and disappear around the curve. On the other side of Maji town, they would start heading down the mountain to the savanna, where the Ethiopian Airlines airplanes landed. From there, they would fly back to America.

That night, I started a letter to my other grandma in Iowa. I wrote, "We all wanted to cry but only Mommy did." Cathy stood beside my chair and said her first sentence over and over. "Grandpa wave his hat."

Grandpa left lots of good memories with us—like the time he made a kite that made everyone who worked on the compound laugh and want a turn trying to make it fly. Tasso, one of the school boys, said he was sure we could send mail to Addis Ababa tied to its tail.

Grandma Kurtz riding a mule

To the end, I never heard Grandma say that I was going to become a fine seamstress some day or that I was a good little girl. But she did tell my mom and dad that they were doing a good job of guiding my determined spirit. "She should go far," she wrote in a letter, "and accomplish much in this world."

TRAVELING "HOME"

My grandparents went back to being unreal. I forgot the names of my cousins. But around the time I turned seven, my mom and dad had some astonishing news. "We're going to go home," Daddy said. "For a year, we'll be on furlough."

Going home? My sisters and I looked with puzzled eyes around our new house. The fat black wood stove in the living room, with a pipe that carried hot sparks up and out the chimney. The new roof that turned into a thunderous drum every time rain pelted down on it—so loud I couldn't hear Joy in the bunk below me even if I leaned over the side of my bed. The porch, where Daddy had helped us put our handprints into the wet cement.

The Kurtz family with their new house

Were we going to build another house? Would Grandpa come back to help?

Mom and Dad thought our questions were funny. Didn't we understand about going home? We would spend the year in Boise, Idaho, which was a city near Grandpa and Grandma's farm. Was Boise farther away than Addis Ababa? Mom told us it was in America. Where we were from.

On June 29, we took off in a big Ethiopian Airlines airplane. By that night, we were in Athens, Greece. From there, we took airplanes to Zurich, Switzerland; Frankfurt, Germany; and Rotterdam, Holland. That's where we got back onto a ship on July 13.

Eight days later, we slid past the Statue of Liberty again.

Everything seemed strange and confusing. One evening, after we had eaten supper in a cafeteria with rows and rows of food, we ran ahead to the elevator, eager to get back to our hotel room because we had discovered something that could be found right in the corner just by turning a knob. Cartoon stories—on television.

By the time our parents caught up with us on our hotel floor, we told them that the elevator operator had asked us, "Where are you from?"

"What did you say?" Dad asked.

I thought about how embarrassing it had been to have the man looking down at us, waiting for an answer, while we had to whisper among ourselves in the corner about what the right answer was. Finally we'd told him, "We're from America."

Mom and Dad went to meetings in the Presbyterian church headquarters at 475 Riverside Drive. I liked to repeat the address, which was almost like a rhyme. No one I knew before had ever had an address.

When the meetings were finished, we got into a big station wagon. Daddy explained that every morning we would drive a hundred miles before breakfast. Every night we would sleep in the house of someone we knew—and we were to be polite, helpful, and well behaved. It would take a few weeks before we'd be in our one-year home.

DISCOVERING THE OREGON TRAIL

As we drove across the United States, we followed about the same route that Carrie Stafford—Daddy's grandma—went on in 1881 when she was six. She crossed the Great Plains in a covered wagon with her family. She picked flowers, gathered cow chips for the fire, and helped watch over her two younger sisters.

Carrie's family settled near the Boise River in Idaho and started to farm the land. A year or two later, a young man in his twenties wandered up looking for work. His French mother was dead. His Scottish father would have nothing to do with him. They had left him with nothing except the difficult name of Hezekiah. (His nickname, Hez, wasn't that much better.) Hez wandered up to Carrie's father and asked him for a job.

"What's your name?" stern George Stafford asked.

"I don't like my name," Hez answered.

George Stafford put a hand scythe in the young man's hands. He said, "Well, come over here and start to work, Billy."

By the end of the day, Hez—ever after known as Billy—had spent many hours cutting alfalfa. He settled in to wait for young Carrie to get old enough to marry him. Their children, including my grandma, grew up along the border of Idaho and Oregon, a dry land where low hills, full of sagebrush, touched the sky.

My fascination with the Oregon Trail started early. In the mid-1800s, dreams of a better life were so powerful that half a million people had turned their backs on cozy houses and said goodbye, knowing they would probably never again see the friends and family they left behind. Men, women, and children who hadn't taken trips longer than a day or two left behind their feather beds, orchards, and farms.

Farmers sold land and bought wagons and oxen, getting ready to walk 2,000 miles. The trip took from four to eight months. Most often, the young and the old walked, day after day. They ran into heat and cold, dust and mud, rocks and rivers. Sometimes, the travelers' own relatives or former friends became enemies.

People woke up to the sounds of whips cracking and men shouting, "Ida ho-ho ho-ho ho." Oxen rumbled into place. People gulped down breakfast—cold beans and coffee—and rubbed their legs and feet. Everyone might be stiff and sore and homesick and a little bit cross, but at least they were alive to chase their dreams for another day.

Some of the travelers kept going all the way over the high Cascade Mountains to the lush and green lands in western Oregon where they could plant orchards, and where crops grew well. Others (like my family) settled in the dry eastern area full of sagebrush and jackrabbits.

The year I was seven, I got to splash in the river where my father used to swim when he was a boy. "Jump," he shouted to us, as we stood on a flat rock staring at the water.

"But Daddy," I called back, "are there crocodiles?"

I played with my cousins on the farm where Daddy grew up driving a farm wagon over the ruts of the Oregon Trail. I ate my grandma's

Jane in America (*second from left*)

homemade jams and doughnuts. (I also got in trouble with her for wearing my cousin's socks to wade in some mud.)

BOISE SECOND GRADER

At our home in the nearby city of Boise, Idaho, everything seemed strange. Gas stations were new. So was snow. Drinking root beer was, too. I didn't understand things like television. When my parents were interviewed on a Boise television station, I sat in the corner of the living room giving them little secret waves and whispering, "Hi, Mommy. Hi Daddy" because I thought they could see me, since I could see them.

But mostly being in the United States was difficult for me. My parents cut my hair short because I hated to sit still and have it brushed. I was impatient in school when the other children in my group read too slowly. Still, one wonderful thing happened.

I finally got a baby brother.

Jane *(standing in middle)* in Boise

When we went back to Ethiopia that summer, we got to take Christopher John.

For now, the word *home* once again meant Maji. Other questions about home would wait until later.

WRITERS THINK ABOUT WRITING

Vivid Details

Good writers are treasure hunters for vivid, interesting details that will pull the reader inside the experience or inside the writer's thoughts.

Sometimes writers can't use their memories or observations to gather good details. That's when research comes in handy. Since I never traveled in a covered wagon, I had to dig for details recorded by people who did.

Lots of the Oregon Trail travelers took the time to write about their adventures in their journals. Even if they weren't sure how to spell the words, they wanted to record what it was like to be a pioneer.

For a while, the land looked almost the same morning, noon, and night. Chimney Rock stuck right up out of the plains, and many pioneers wrote about climbing up to leave their names and messages there for later travelers.

One man described a woman who "after having kneaded her dough ... held an umbrella over the fire and her skillit ... for near two hours and baked bread enough to give us a verry plentiful supper." At Soda Springs, people were fascinated by the bubbling waters. A man wrote, "the Sody Spring is aquite acuriosity there is agreat many of them Just boiling rite up out of the ground take alitle sugar and desolve it in alittle water and then dip up acup full." Once the sugar was dissolved, he added, it was important to drink quickly before the water lost its bubbly gas.

1) Notice the ways I used those journal writings to create the cooking scene on page 43, the rock-climbing scene on pages 59–61, and the scene that involves Soda Springs, starting on page 104 of *I'm Sorry, Almira Ann.*

2) Take a look at a piece of writing you've been working on and ask yourself whether research might give you some useful details. Some young writers I worked with, for example, did research on the following things that were helpful for their fiction:

   a) the insides of various kinds of caves;
   b) what a cheetah looks like when it runs;
   c) the way soldiers dressed during Roman times;
   d) what children eat for breakfast in China.

3) Illustrators do research, too. Susan Havice writes, "As soon as the manuscript of *I'm Sorry, Almira Ann* arrived, I sat down in a very comfortable chair to read and reread Jane Kurtz's wonderful story about a young girl, her family, and friends heading west. Soon my fingers were grabbing a pencil so I could sketch the ideas that were tumbling out. A few things were new to me including Sarah climbing Chimney Rock. What did that look like? Chimney Rock isn't in a lot of American history books, but my husband teaches

a course in Westward Movement, so I could borrow from his large collection of books to find it. He also had source materials for ox bows, buckets, wagons, and more." Sometimes trying to draw a picture of a scene lets you know what you don't know! Sometimes, a fascinating picture can be a source of inspiration and unexpected detail.

Organization

Good writers organize, working hard to find the best structure for a piece and a compelling beginning, middle, and end.

I first wrote *I'm Sorry, Almira Ann* as a picture book. The manuscript was seven pages long. An editor suggested that I turn it into a chapter book, which I did. This was the old beginning:

> In the middle of the afternoon, the exhausted oxen smelled water.
> At first, they tossed their heads and snorted. Sarah thought her eyes must be crazy from the dazzle of shiny dried lakes. But then Father turned and looked back at her, sweat smeared on his face. "The Green River," he called.
> "Oh yes," Mother whispered and grabbed Chatworth's hand.
> The oxen stumbled into a clumsy gallop.
> "Come on!" Father yelled.
> Even Lucy the cow trotted.
> But Sarah's throat was full of dust. She watched the wagons lurch by. Maybe she would never catch up. They would go on to Oregon without her, and she would never see any of them again. It would serve her right.

1) Writers often try to drop the reader right into the middle of the story, which means there is often a sense of mystery in an opening that the reader knows will slowly become better understood. List all the questions you can think of that are raised by that opening.
2) Often writers try several different beginnings to a story before they settle on one. Look at the new beginning, in the published book *I'm Sorry, Almira Ann*. Where does the old beginning take place? Where does the new one take place? Why do you think I made such a drastic change? What questions are raised by the new opening?
3) Look at the opening of one of your pieces of writing. Does it drop the reader right into the middle? Does it make the reader curious? What questions might the reader be asking that you, the writer, intend to answer as the piece goes along?

4) Look at page 96 of *I'm Sorry, Almira Ann* to see where I eventually did use the old opening of the picture book. If you've written something you like but decide it isn't your best beginning, you may still find another place where it belongs.

Write What You Know: *Mr. Bones, Johnny Appleseed, What Columbus Found*

One day I was asked to do a school presentation for second graders who were writing their memoirs. The librarian asked me if I could show them any written connections to the year I was a second grader. I dug through my notes, jottings, and memories to figure out if I could trace anything in my books to that year.

The year I was seven, my little brother came into my life. He was charming and fuzzy and I liked him immensely.

But I also developed another fascination that year, and this second thing wasn't charming or fuzzy at all.

When my family was driving from New York City to Oregon, we camped at Dinosaur National Monument in Utah. I saw something that had always intrigued me.

Bones. Big old bones.

The bones I stared at when I was in second grade had a long history. In 1909, a paleontologist named Earl Douglass, who worked for the Carnegie Museum, began poking around the rocks of northeastern Utah. Long ago, that land had a wide river with dinosaurs living beside

Chris, my baby brother

it. Their bones ended up in the riverbed, covered with sand and gravel. Slowly, over the ages, the bones had turned to fossils—and Douglass uncovered thousands of them to ship to the museum back in Pittsburgh, Pennsylvania.

In 1915, President Woodrow Wilson decided that this quarry of dinosaur bones should become Dinosaur National Monument. Today, outside the visitor center, people line up to study a tall wall where the rock face has been chipped away to reveal more than 1,500 fossil bones lying in their places as if waiting to be dug out by Earl Douglass or another paleontologist.

As a skinny seven-year-old explorer, I stood in the reddish dust with a hot wind swirling up around my legs and gaped at those bones at Dinosaur National Monument, amazed to think that plant-eating sauropods with their long, snaky necks—the biggest creatures to walk on land—had planted their enormous feet right there in that place. Exactly where I was standing.

The small, metal replica of this creature in the gift shop made me gulp with longing. I thought I would be contented forever if I could own it.

Since there were a lot of children in our family, my parents were not inclined to give in to any of our pleadings that we should be allowed to buy souvenirs at any of our many stops. They said no to raccoon caps and turquoise necklaces and polished rocks and small candies. I don't know why they let me buy the dinosaur, but I vowed I would never lose it, even when I was eighty years old. Sadly, I was no good at keeping such vows. But I never did lose the memory of the dinosaur—or my interest.

MY CHILDREN DISCOVER DINOSAURS

Many years later, when our children were old enough, my husband and I decided our summer camping vacation route should include Dinosaur National Monument.

My oldest son, David, had been attracted to dinosaurs as soon as he could crawl. After we got home from Dinosaur National Monument, he learned complicated dinosaur names and wanted to have his favorite nonfiction descriptions read over and over. His ability to remember their complicated names reminded me of my little brother who, before he could read, would stand by a chart of fish and proudly point to the

David and Jonathan at Dinosaur National Monument

fish that had the longest name of all. "Huma-huma-nuka-nuka-op-wa," my brother would say, astonishing everyone.

In the same way, David would sit on my lap and point to pictures and say *ankylosaurus* and *archaeopteryx* and *seismosaurus* and *velociraptor*. He played dinosaur games with Jonathan. "I'm apatosaurus," he said.

"I'm Booga," Jonathan said promptly.

"There's no such thing as a booga. We're playing like real."

I wrote this comment down in my idea book. In those days, I was reading aloud about dinosaurs all the time. And, of course, I also tried my hand at writing dinosaur stories.

One day, Jonathan frowned at David, who was playing dinosaur, and then asked, "Mom, does triceratops only know push and jab and roar?"

I jotted down that comment, too, in my idea book. More dinosaur stories came pouring out. I was following one of the first rules for writers: write about what you know about and care about.

None of my dinosaur stories ever got published. But I kept collecting lines. "Jonathan's making up stories and crashing them into mine," David complained. I wrote it down.

BUNNIES AND BONES

It took about twenty years, but I finally did get a chance to write a dinosaur book. An editor I had met at a Society for Children's Books and Illustrators conference asked me if I would be willing to try my hand at writing a nonfiction easy-to-read book for Aladdin Books.

Choosing the subject of my first book turned out to be easy. I would write about Johnny Appleseed because so many kindergarten and first-grade classrooms I visited were doing apple units. While I was walking on the treadmill, the opening line popped into my mind. I scribbled it onto a small card.

I was off! Even after I had a draft—when I got to the stage where I needed to count syllables in each line—I was still having fun.

But what should I write about next?

My editor suggested Beatrix Potter, the author of *Peter Rabbit*. I remembered one year when my sisters and I practiced to put on a play of *Peter Rabbit*. I thought about the rabbits I saw every day on my walks in Kansas. Perfect.

I did research and started to write.

Beatrix Potter was a small, shy girl.
She lived in London.
She never went to school.

What an intriguing life this little girl had. When she was fifteen years old, she wrote in code so that no one could read her secret diaries. Until her little brother, Bertram, was born, her only companions were the small creatures—mice and the like—that she was allowed to keep in her room. She cared for them tenderly and, after they died, studied their tiny bones.

But the committee who looked at my manuscript decided she wasn't the right person for the next ready-to-read book by Jane Kurtz. My editor delivered the bad news.

If not Beatrix, then who?

I tried (and tossed away) many other ideas before one of the members of my writers' group, Jennifer Jacobson—who was a teacher before she became an author—asked, "What about the man who discovered the first Tyrannosaurus Rex skeleton?"

Ooooo. Dinosaurs.

As soon as I got home from the writing retreat, I ordered some books so I could read about Barnum Brown. I uncovered interesting tidbits. Barnum Brown wore a topcoat, a snappy hat, and a tie even when the folks around him were Montana cowboys. He was an excellent ballroom dancer. His wife, Lilian, said they were "rainbow-chasing," following yellow, gray, red, purple, and green sedimentary rocks, when they hunted fossils in Burma.

> Some of the tidbits never made their way into my book. For instance, Barnum Brown started his paleontology studies at the University of Kansas, the state where I was living when I wrote the book about him. His mother named him after P.T. Barnum, the showman who created the Barnum and Bailey Circus. She hoped the name would encourage him to think of big things he could do with his life.

I read and read about dinosaur discoveries. Luckily, my interest in these books and the dinosaur hunters and their discoveries stretched back to my childhood—and to my children's lives. That made the research extra fun.

> Mary Haverfield, who illustrated *Mr. Bones,* also had a son who once loved dinosaurs. When she started to work, she already had stacks of books sitting around the house that she could study to see exactly what T-Rex bones looked like. Like me, she needed to find out about the real Barnum Brown and was determined to pin down details, such as what kind of hat he wore.
>
> She went to the library and hauled home stacks of books. She also looked at photographs on the Internet and printed out lots of pictures from an online source. With all of her research around her and buzzing in her head, she was ready to start final sketches. Her model for Barnum Brown was her husband. He let her use him even though her drawings made him appear older and heavier than he is in real life.

PUMPKIN DISCOVERIES

While searching for another topic to use for a third easy-to-read book, I found a topic that also rang bells in my brain from long ago. It took me back to the days when I went to school for the first time and learned to say a rhyme with my classmates. "In 1492, Columbus sailed the ocean blue."

In high school, I found out that Columbus didn't discover America at all. In 2005, I found out that when he reached the North American continent, he stumbled onto something that was already being culti-vated there, something that played a big part in my children's lives.

Pumpkins.

When my children were young, we loved things that were orange and round and sprouted on vines. David grew a 200-pound squash one year, and I cut it up and put pieces of it in my cooking until everyone protested. They carved pumpkins. I roasted the seeds—and sometimes I sat nearby and wrote down my children's comments in my idea book.

> Ouch. I'm never going to be able to use my right hand again.
> Did you see the way it opened?
> Pull up your sleeves.
> Oooh. Ugh. Ooooh.
> Gunky junk.
> Look at all the seeds.
> Gross.
> We're taking the brains out of a pumpkin.
> Do you hate it or love it? Love it.
> I'll bet there's a hundred seeds.
> Let's count them.
> We can't count every single slimy gunky seed.
> How does a pumpkin patch get started, anyway?

Those years of having pumpkins around the house, I never really thought about their history and how they had become such a symbol of Thanksgiving. I didn't consider writing about pumpkins until my editor asked me if I knew anyone famous who had anything to do with them.

Authors certainly don't need to have a longtime interest in the things they write about. Anything that makes you curious or fascinates you is a good topic to explore for writing. But if you can write about something you have always been crazy about, it certainly doesn't hurt.

WRITERS THINK ABOUT WRITING

> **Ideas**
> Good writers gather ideas that are interesting, focused, and based on things the writer knows about and cares about.

1. When I wrote books about a dinosaur hunter and about pump-kins, I was writing about things that had popped up in my idea books for years because I'd been interested in them for a long

time. Make a list. What do you know a lot about? Is there anything on your list you don't care much about? If so, cross it off.

2. Mary Haverfield says, "One of my favorite parts of all my jobs is the research in the beginning. I always learn something new." On your list, is there anything that you could research that would help you write about that topic?

3. Show your list to a teacher or a friend. Ask if there's something they'd love to read about. These are some of the ways that writers figure out their next ideas.

Rhythm and Beat

Good writers listen to the rhythms of sentences and pay attention to how one sentence flows into and fits with the next.

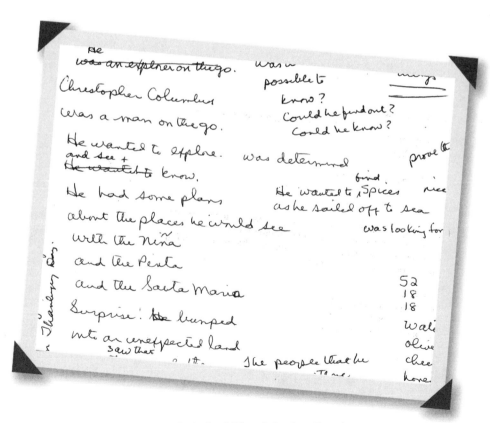

Rough draft of *What Columbus Found*

1. Often a one-word or two-word sentence can add a crisp punch to your writing. Try tapping out the rhythm of these sentences, for instance:

   But what he hunted, people wanted just about as much as gold. Bones. Big old bones.

2. Look at a piece of writing you are working on. Alternate markers of three different colors and color your sentences. (Use one color for the first sentence, the second color for the second sentence, the third color for the third sentence, and then start over again.) You should be able to tell at a glance whether your sentences are all about the same length. If they are, give your reader more variety.

Revising Ideas and Conventions

Good writers revise bravely and boldly, making big changes, and also revise patiently and carefully, making tiny changes.

Study my rough draft (page 77) for *What Columbus Found.* Compare it with the finished version. What parts changed the most?

The Hot Savanna: The Story Behind
Water Hole Waiting

My childhood was full of comings and goings.

The Kurtz family had adventures on those journeys from the United States to Ethiopia and back again, but we also had adventures—sometimes wonderful ones, sometimes scary ones—every time we took an airplane out of Maji.

Being inside an Ethiopian Airlines DC-3 was always an adventure. First, I had to climb up a short ladder into the back and step inside what felt a little like a giant tin can. The floor sloped steeply. When I managed to make my way to my bucket seat and fasten the seat belt, I had nothing to lean back on except the side of the airplane. Once the propellers started, we had to shout if we wanted to talk, and the walls of the plane vibrated and trembled.

The airplane made several stops. In Jimma, the bumps were gentle as the airplane landed on the black tarmac, but in Gore and Mizan

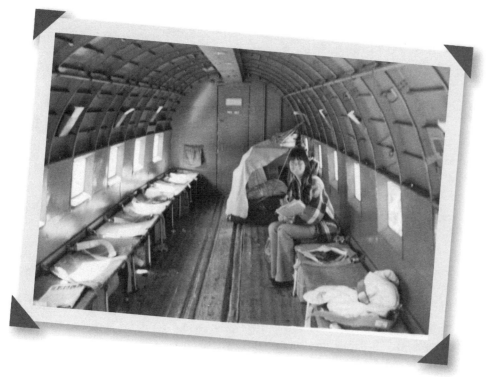

Cathy in the bucket seat on a trip to Maji

Jane on a mule near "Down on Both Sides"

Teferi, we bounced or skidded on grassy, sometimes muddy airstrips. Cargo was loaded on and off—coffee bags that smelled wonderful and dried animal skins that didn't.

When the airplane finally got close to Maji, the only place flat enough to land was the grassy, hot savanna. From there, we still had to ride thirty-two miles, going up 8,000 feet on a slow, bumpy road. The trip took one day by Jeep, two days by mule.

A LONG, TOUGH TREK

My dad had to make that trip many times, usually driving the old Jeep that he and the workmen tried their best to keep running. When he took us along, we waited for the interesting places. There was the flat spot we called "Super Highway," where we could stand up in the Jeep and let the wind blow our hair straight back. Another place was "Down on Both Sides," where I sometimes dreamed the Jeep would plunge off the edge and tumble for miles to the plains below.

The Ethiopians called that spot *Nifas Birr,* "Gate of the Wind."

Another dramatic spot on the road to Washa Wuha was a streambed where tsetse flies swarmed and bit us so hard they raised red welts. Those flies caused sleeping sickness in the mules. We used our sock monkeys to slap wildly at the flies.

Sometimes Daddy went alone to pick up guests who wanted to see Maji. Other times, he transported parts of machines or other supplies. Two years after our furlough in Boise, he drove my mom down the mountain so she could fly to the hospital in Addis Ababa. My youngest sister, Jan, was born there.

The savanna was a fascinating place. *Washa Wuha* meant "Cave of Water," but usually the only water I saw was a bit of warm liquid that I slurped from a smelly canvas canteen. My sisters and I wandered through the crackling, dry grasses looking for quartz rocks and gathering them up as treasures. When we got too hot, we rested in the shade of the airplane wing, smelling the fuel and listening to the shouts of men loading and unloading.

But the savanna was also our vacation spot because it was the place where the animals roamed. Daddy navigated the Jeep through the crackling grasses that bent as if they were bowing to royalty. I liked to imagine I was the princess they bowed for. Hundreds of grazing animals galloped or munched off to the sides. Daddy stopped and let us put our fingers into an elephant footstep. Another time, he took us into the prickly bushes at night and used lights to show us nocturnal animals, including tiny bush babies.

Sometimes we camped nearby at a place we called German Wuha. On those trips, we drove through miles and miles of grasses, watching the notch in the hills that showed Daddy how to navigate the Jeep. We saw so many ostriches, flapping their legs in what looked to us like an awkward, sideways bend, that we eventually got bored. "Can't we see anything but zebras and antelopes and ostriches?" one of us would finally ask.

German Wuha was where we learned to fish. One evening, the fish bit anything we threw in the water, including empty hooks. German Wuha was where Daddy thrilled us with the story of how he swam around a bend of the river and came face to face with a water buffalo. German Wuha was where—one exciting time when Daddy left us for a few days—I managed to set the tent on fire with my little brother in it. I wrote about it in my first diary.

January 4—It was an exciting ha ha day. All day we swam and panned for gold. We really thought we had some. Us kids wanted to open another can of fish but Daddy had the can opener. So we decided to go ask for one from the police. We had to say *kora kora mukeffucha affellegallo*. They said *huh?* I repeated it but when I got to the 2nd word I couldn't think of it so we got all goofed up + didn't get the can opener. Last night quite late Chris called "Janie." He was in my tent + I was outside. I said "Wait a minute." He kept calling + then he shouted "Come quick." I walked over there and the back of the tent was flaming. I tried to blow it then screamed for Mommy. She took one look + yelled "The bucket of water." When that was empty we used the water the dishes were in.

Although my report ends there, I remember my mom tossing the pan of dishwater—dishes and all—onto the tent. It didn't help. The tent was ruined (and my diary had a burnt spot on it forever after) but we did save Chris!

Camping at The Rock

RUINED PLANS

On another fateful trip, we had three guests staying with us, and the plan was to take them and Aunt Ruth on a camping trip to a huge whale of a rock near Washa Wuha. The next morning Aunt Ruth was going to get on the plane to Addis Ababa, while we picked up three more guests, took them camping at German Wuha, and drove with them back to Maji.

Where I lived, plans hardly ever worked the way they should.

First of all, we got two flat tires on the way down. After Daddy crawled out from under the Jeep the second time, he said, "Looks like the differential joint of the front drive shaft is going out." I didn't know what that meant, but I did understand his next words. "We'd better camp here and let me think this over until morning."

"Does that mean we can't go to The Rock after all?" I complained.

My mom shushed me. "The most important thing is that Aunt Ruth has to catch her airplane. We're not going to take the chance she might have to walk across the burning plains."

Daddy always had to be creative in this place with no stores. While he was thinking about what to do, Mom pointed out that at least there was a stream nearby. She warned us, "It will probably be scummy," but it wasn't. Heavy rains that year had left it full of water. All six of us kids

One of the old Maji Jeeps

jumped in and started making a dam so we could have a little swimming pool.

By suppertime, Daddy had made his decision. He told us he had considered driving back to Maji and getting a differential joint out of the old Jeep. Instead, he was going to tell the mule driver who would be getting the mailbags from the airplane and carrying them up the mountain to ask the workman back in Maji to take out the part and send it down to us.

Mom made nervous noises. What if we and all our guests got stranded in a hot, waterless area full of biting tsetse flies?

Daddy told her not to worry.

Sure enough—the next day, we made it to Washa Wuha. Three guests got off the airplane and Aunt Ruth got on. "I wonder what kind of wild-goose chase they think they're embarking on," Mom whispered. Nine of us were already lined up at the Jeep. How would we squeeze three more in?

As my mom later wrote in a letter, Daddy figured out a seat of sorts for everyone, and "miraculously," we all fit in. "We lost the road several times going across those grassy plains," she added, "but found it at the crucial time, especially the one time when we were working our way through an area of thickly grown bushes and thorn trees on the bank of a dry stream. We got to the camping spot and had to pick the site of the tents minutes before we were plunged into darkness."

But when we reached German Wuha, what joy! Unlike the cold, swift rivers of Maji—that plunged into waterfalls if we followed them long enough—this river poked along, wide and brown and warm. We rode air mattresses down the ripples and made up games that we showed off to Mom and Dad and our guests.

Jane with Cathy on an air mattress

Somehow, Mom always figured out how to divide the food into twelve portions for two main meals and one teatime every day. German Wuha was always fun.

But then there was the trip home. We saw so many more ostriches, with their funny, flapping legs, that we eventually barely gave them a glance. We sang every song we knew and quoted our favorite poems to each other to make the time pass. We dangled our legs out the sides of the Jeep to try to give ourselves more room.

Then the Jeep started climbing. The first clue that heavy rains had fallen was that one of the dry riverbeds we'd crossed was now a lively stream. We all got out for a cooling wade. Chris and Jan, who were toddlers, threw off their clothes and lay down in the water.

Mom wrote, "We finally pulled the cherubs, ourselves, and the stuck trailer and Jeep out of the river and went on our way. Every once in a while we would find ourselves going through areas of thick thorn trees, and those of us currently riding on the sides with legs hanging out would make a mighty scramble to get them and ourselves pulled in.

With twelve in the Jeep, it was sort of a necessity that certain parts of some hang out whenever possible!"

At the stream where we had camped, we met the messenger from Maji, who was not only carrying the part we needed for the Jeep but also cinnamon rolls and carrots and cabbage from the garden, sent down by the nurse in the compound. We tore into the rolls, gave the carrots a quick rinse in the stream, and devoured them whole. Even the cabbage leaves tasted luscious, crisp, and crunchy in the heat. Our cheese came in cans, and Mom opened one, finishing off the meal.

Mom wrote that she had never seen the road in such bad shape. "The rain had washed every vestige of dirt from between the boulders, and we just had to creep over them, leaping up from one to another." In the most treacherous places, all of the passengers got out and walked, while Daddy pushed the gas pedal to the floor and zoomed up and around and over the road.

Mom always wanted to clobber Daddy when he would happily announce that we were at the halfway mark. This time, we stared at each other, thinking it couldn't possibly be true. We had already bounced and bumped for so long that surely Maji must be around the next corner. But it was true, and even though darkness was almost on us, we ate a little

more bread and some cookies, wrapped up in sweaters, jackets, and blankets, and went on, hoping the worst of the road was behind us.

Before long, we came to a slope that had a spring tucked away. It had turned into a mass of slippery, muddy rocks. "We'll never make it up pulling the trailer," Mom said. "And there are steeper climbs yet to come. We'd better just leave the trailer here."

Daddy didn't think that was a good idea. What if we had to stop further on and needed the tents and sleeping bags? At the very best, if we got all the way to Maji, he would have to turn around the next day and plod wearily all the way back for the trailer.

"What to do?" Mom wrote in her letter. "We were as stuck as I've ever been stuck."

Daddy was hardly ever without ideas. First he put rocks behind the trailer wheels so it wouldn't roll backwards ("over the abyss"). All of the women helped lift and hold the trailer, while Daddy roared in the Jeep up the slope. As soon as he could stop, he tied one end of a mighty rope to the back of the Jeep and the other end onto the trailer.

I watched with scared eyes. Joy was chewing on her fingernails. "All right!" Daddy shouted.

Zoom. The jeep lurched off. It got to a curve and went around. The trailer hadn't moved yet. Wait! It was moving. But what if it went flying off the curve instead of around the corner after the Jeep?

I squatted down and put my head on my arms so I wouldn't have to watch. "Come on," Mom said, tugging me up. "We have to catch up."

When we got to the next almost-level stop, Daddy was busy getting the Jeep and trailer hooked back together. "Of course it worked," he said calmly. "I've had to do this before."

We went on, as Mom wrote, "exceedingly crowded by this time, for our legs had to be inside or be frozen off," until the next hill, when we had to repeat the rope trick all over again. Mom wrote that she worried the trip "must be an interminable nightmare" to our guests, "but the further we went the higher our spirits soared in spite of the aching weariness of it all and the dread of the possibility that we'd still have to pitch the tents in that expanse of mud and rocks."

For hours we ground on in the dark. The brakes failed, and my father had to manage the Jeep by downshifting gears. My sister Janice fell asleep on my mom's lap. I let Joy droop her head down on me in the back and didn't dare complain about how sore I was from sitting on the hard Jeep bench with no padding.

Near midnight, my mom wrote, "we groaned down the hill into the small stream on the outskirts of Maji, and when the engine gasped the signal that it was out of gas, we about laughed ourselves into hysterics.

The town of Maji

There was another can of gas in the trailer under the roped-down canvas, so it took only fifteen or twenty minutes to get down to it, swallow a couple of mouthfuls in the process of siphoning it into the can for pouring it into the tank, and chug on. About this time Janice awoke from her peaceful, uncomprehending slumbers, looked around, and grinningly started her current chorus of 'Happity, happity, happity.' Within a half hour we staggered numbly into the house."

Sometimes it was all a little too much adventure for me. But years later, my brother and I took our memories of the hot savanna and the animals that are drawn to the cool water and wrote one of my favorite picture books, *Water Hole Waiting*.

WRITERS THINK ABOUT WRITING

Rhythm and Beat
Good writers listen to the rhythms of sentences and pay attention to how one sentence flows into and fits with the next.

One easy way to make sentences flow more gracefully is to make sure all of your sentences aren't long, aren't short, or aren't medium-length.

1) Count the number of words in the first sentence of *Water Hole Waiting*. Count the number in the second sentence. Now count the third. Which one is long, which is medium, and which is short? Practice reading the first page out loud until you have the rhythm as smooth as you possibly can.

2) Study a piece of writing you're working on. Pick a few sentences that you can count in the same way. Try to make some sentences long (perhaps doing sentence combining) and look for a good place where you want the reader to feel the punch of a short sentence.

Word Choice

Good writers use words that are specific and interesting, words with sparkle and pizzazz.

Some writing programs emphasize using adjectives and adverbs to paint a picture in the reader's mind. There's nothing wrong with using an occasional startling, amazing adjective or adverb, but most of your sparkle should come from interesting verbs.

1) Make a list of the verbs you find in *Water Hole Waiting*.

2) Brainstorm to fill up a paper or white board with interesting verbs. (You could also do this with your whole class.) Think about interesting movements. How does a tiger move? How does a bear move? How does the wind move? Waves? Willow trees?

3) With a piece of writing you're working on, challenge yourself to use at least three interesting verbs. Be playful and have fun. Morning can't really slink and lick up shadows, but it's an effective writing technique to take something inanimate (like a rock) and give it the characteristics of a person or an animal.

Revising Ideas and Conventions

Good writers revise bravely and boldly, making big changes, and also revise patiently and carefully, making tiny changes.

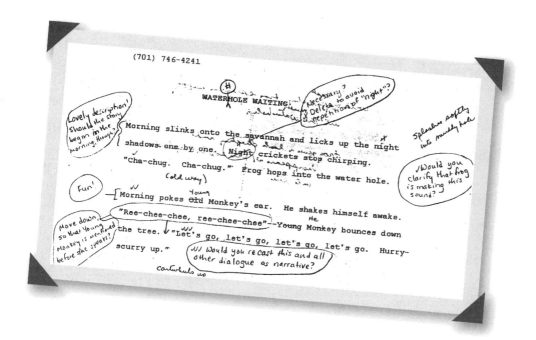

Look at the editor's revision suggestions for the opening of *Water Hole Waiting*. Some of the tasks were easy. For instance, check to see how we responded to the editor's request, "Would you clarify that frog is making this sound?"

Some of the tasks were hard. When the editor said, "Would you recast this and all other dialogue as narrative," it wasn't easy to see a new way. Here are some of the notes we scribbled as we were trying to figure it out. See if you can spot ideas or phrases that ended up in the final version.

fluid and smooth as a river of ooze
They leap, they bound, they end up on the ground.
Young monkey thinks it's time to take a drink
A great time for ... repeat?
Ditch Old Monkey completely?
But (wait) the water hole is full of cranky hippopotami (work with sky)
Whip whap
Slip slap
Wait! Old Monkey pulls her back
Grabs her tail? paw yawn jaw

School Times: Leading to *Jakarta Missing*

In the early days, reading, writing, and arithmetic all happened right where I lived.

The school outside the compound was for Ethiopian students in the first through the sixth grades, and the instruction was all in Amharic. Some of the first graders were almost six feet tall. Wherever the Presbyterians had started schools in the southwest part of Ethiopia, there were boys and young men who were determined to grab the chance to get an education, even if they had to walk barefoot for hours or work until nightfall cutting grass around the school and the compound with a small sickle to earn money for supplies.

Jane (*on left*) reading

LEARNING TO READ IN MAJI

I wanted to go to school.

Since classes in the school were all conducted in Amharic, my mom started to teach my six-year-old sister, Carolyn, at home. I hung around and watched with jealous eyes. Carolyn had already gotten to go to real kindergarten while we lived in Addis Ababa—and her kindergarten teacher even gave her a beautiful doll that she named Alice. Now she got to have even more school.

Young men working at the compound

"Me too," I said, so many times that my mom gave in.

When we had finished our oatmeal or cracked wheat cereal for breakfast, Mom would say, "Wash your hands, Carolyn. It's time for school."

"Do I have to go to school, too?" I would ask.

"Only if you want to."

"No, Mom," I would insist. "Tell me I *have* to."

I was stubbornly determined to be a real student. By the time my sixth birthday rolled around, my mom wrote in a letter to her mom in Iowa, "Janie continues to storm right along. She can read third-grade material with hardly a stumble."

Carolyn often complained to my parents that her little sisters were copying her. It probably didn't help to know that my mother was typing things like this in her letters: "Janie has quite a mind for memorizing. She gets things learned as fast as Carolyn does and seems to remember them longer."

She also wrote:

"I believe Janie is going to be reading all of the first-grade material by the end of the year for she still works at it as hard as ever and is so proud of her achievement. Carolyn goes along very nicely in it too, but it is good for her to have Janie just a jump behind to really spur her on."

Maybe my mom thought it was good for her, but Carolyn did not particularly appreciate noticing me always just a jump behind. She thought

I was trying to compete with her, and she didn't like it. But from my point of view, my older sister was wondrous—beautiful, smart, good, with golden hair. I wanted to keep up with her, hoping she would let me into her world.

I was also so eager to have books to read that I probably made a pest of myself. Soon my mother reported, "Carolyn and Janie work hard on their school every day and are coming along beautifully. Janie is patiently waiting on Carolyn to finish the first regular primer so she can start it, and I am having her drill in the meantime on some of the harder words she's running into all the time now."

Carolyn and Jane, the two oldest daughters

OFF TO BOARDING SCHOOL

By the time we had our furlough year in Boise, Idaho, I was such a whiz at reading that my parents thought perhaps they should put me in the third grade, even though I was only seven. One of Daddy's brothers was a principal and his wife was a teacher, so they gave me a standardized test. When Aunt Idamary realized that one of the questions had me stumped because I didn't know what a picket fence was, she took me outside to show me. Then she told my parents I had other kinds of catching up to do and should probably stick with second grade.

A huge change came when we returned to Ethiopia. My parents, Joy, Cathy, Chris, and I all got on an Ethiopian Airlines DC-3 and flew

When Carolyn was in Maji for a vacation, all four sisters and
our baby brother, Chris, were together

back to Maji. But Carolyn stayed in Addis Ababa. She was going to be a
fifth grader at a brand-new boarding school, the Good Shepherd
School, started by the Presbyterian, Mennonite, Lutheran, and Baptist
churches for families working in Ethiopia.

I missed Carolyn dreadfully. Sometimes I was afraid for her—like
when rebels tried to overthrow the emperor that year. Other times, I
was envious, and I definitely felt I belonged with her. Wherever my
older sister went, I wanted to go, too.

It was a dismal year without my older sister.

Carolyn was able to spend three months at home during the
rainy season months of June, July, and August. By then, I knew that
I'd be going to boarding school when she returned in September. I
spent lots of hours bent over all of my clothes—every piece of under-
wear, every sock, every shirt, every pair of pants, every dress—sewing
name tags onto everything. Jane Kurtz. Jane Kurtz. Jane Kurtz. Those
black letters on the little white strips went by over and over and over
again.

HOMESICKNESS AND GAMES

For my parents, those were the years of the dragging feet and sagging hearts. I had tangled feelings. Now the three other bunks in my bedroom weren't filled with my sisters but with girls my own age. And, oh, the delicious thrill of having a library. I found such treats there. *Lorna Doone.* Not only *Little Women,* but all of the other books by Louisa May Alcott. *The Five Little Peppers and How They Grew.* Whenever I could, I charged to those shelves—and if I couldn't find a book I hadn't read, I was happy to read one over again.

It was exciting to have friends to play with, double on the big swings, taking turns pumping, soaring so high that our stomachs jumped into our mouths and I almost thought we could go flying all the way around in a huge circle. Games came and went: tether ball, marbles, jump rope, and roller skating. In the evenings, long lines stretched in front of the dorm. "Red Rover, Red Rover, let Janie come over." In one of those games, I smacked into one of the big kids and ended up with a black eye.

But something not so happy tagged at our heels. Homesickness. Many nights, sniffling sounds came from pillows as ten-year-olds cried, missing parents and pets and siblings and special blankets. At times, to

Dormitory at Good Shepherd School

keep the bleak feelings away, we stayed awake and chattered until the dorm father knocked on the door and delivered the punishment for talking after lights out—"No dessert tomorrow."

Oh well, we always said. Maybe it would be tapioca anyway. Fish eyes and glue.

PASADENA JUNIOR HIGH

I continued going to the Good Shepherd School until I was in the eighth grade. That is when my family went back to America for a year's furlough in Pasadena, California. As usual, I liked my classes. I had chances to learn things I'd never known anything about when I was chosen for a before-school Madrigal group and learned tennis in gym. But going to junior high with about 2,000 students, after I was used to having a small school of about 200 students in twelve grades, was painful in some ways. I ate lunch by myself and often felt too shy and self-conscious to walk across the outside lunchroom—even to buy my beloved packet of puffed cheese munchies. Worst of all were the times when kids asked, "You grew up in Africa? Did you see Tarzan?"

After the year in Pasadena my family returned to Ethiopia. Good Shepherd School was my school until I left high school after my junior year, when I was seventeen, because I was eager to join my older sister in college.

BECOMING A TEACHER

I've spent a lot of my adult life in classrooms. My favorite job after I graduated from college was being an educator—a writing teacher, a third- and fourth-grade teacher, and a director—at Carbondale New School in Carbondale, Illinois. When my own kids were toddlers and my family lived in Trinidad, Colorado, I adored teaching English to high-school students a few hours a day. After we moved to Grand Forks, North Dakota, I went back to school to earn my master's degree at the University of North Dakota, and then taught writing classes in the English department for ten years.

What would you want to be if you weren't a writer? people ask me.

A teacher, I say. In fact, I've spent many years of my life as a teacher and still like talking about writing with students and teachers in school visits.

SCHOOL DAYS FOR MY CHILDREN

So, you might wonder . . . do I have any bad memories of school?
Yes.

It wasn't always happy times when my own kids were in school.
Since I had loved school so much, I didn't expect—or always know
what to say—when my children had school years when they were
unhappy. When my son David was in junior high, one day he and I
argued over whether he should buy a pair of expensive jeans. I said it
was silly to spend that much money just for a label. He looked at me
and said, "Mom, you don't know what it's like in junior high."

I thought for a minute. *Oh,* I realized. *I* don't *know what it's like in
junior high.*

After that, I made more of an effort to go to all of my children's
sports games, plays, and musical concerts, so I could see for myself what
their schools were like. It was easy to make connections with my daughter's interests. One year when I was chair of the library committee, her
librarian told me, "Rebekah has checked out *Little Women* so many
times, I told her maybe she should leave it for some other little girl."
So I bought my daughter her own copy of the book, as my parents
would have done for me. Her love of stories—reading them and acting
them out—never went away.

My childhood often left me feeling like an outsider in the United
States. I'd never watched a football game until my own sons played on
teams. At first, I didn't like sitting and not knowing the rules, feeling
confused and lost. But my middle child, Jonathan, was athletic. He
wanted to play every sport that came along. When he played baseball,
his team won the state championship. When he played football, he
became the quarterback. By high school, he decided his favorite sport
was basketball.

One year, the basketball coach at Jonathan's high school gathered
the kids together who had been on the sophomore team. He told them
there wouldn't be room for everyone on the junior varsity team, gave
them a sheet with goals on it, and challenged them to shoot the basketball 20,000 times over the summer break.

All that summer, we heard thumps and swishes. When Jonathan
added up his numbers at the end, he had shot the basketball 60,000
times. He jumped right over junior varsity and became a starter on the
varsity team.

That year, in between watching basketball games, I finished writing
the novel that has more of my real childhood memories than any

other, *Jakarta Missing*. The main character is partly patterned on me and partly on my story-loving daughter. Boarding school showed up in the story—and so did all those basketball games I was watching. In fact, I dedicated it to Jonathan, who was so determined to reach his dreams and goals that he shot his basketball 60,000 times.

Ironically, as scenes took shape in my mind and I concentrated on one of the novelist's main jobs—show, don't tell—I ended up pulling many of my specific details from a country I'd never visited as a child: Kenya. During the years I was working on *Jakarta Missing* I twice visited my older sister, who was then living in Kenya and working in the Sudan.

From the flowers that spilled over the gates along the road to the "Fasten Seatbelt" sign on the Kenya Airways flight, I mixed observational details with memory details and cooked the stew that became a book.

WRITERS THINK ABOUT WRITING

Interesting Ideas

Good writers gather ideas that are interesting, focused, and based on things the writer knows about and cares about.

A novel needs lots of interesting ideas. From the things I wrote in this chapter, you can puzzle out where each of these early ideas of my novel came from—observation, memory, research, or imagination.

1) Dakar is missing her older sister, Jakarta.
2) Dakar and Jakarta have been growing up in East Africa.
3) Their mother grew up in North Dakota.
4) A bomb has just gone off in Nairobi, the capital of Kenya.
5) Jakarta is a great basketball player.
6) Dakar and Jakarta have been in boarding school.
7) Their father believes he needs to make the world better for people.
8) Dakar doesn't know what to say when kids ask her about Africa.
9) Dakar misses the Italian ice cream in Kenya.
10) Jakarta was born in Indonesia.

Look at a piece of your own writing to figure out whether you rely on one way of gathering details and if you should experiment with another way.

Word Choice

Good writers use words that are specific and interesting, words with sparkle and pizzazz.

In Chapter One, Dakar and her American friend Melanie look at a catalog and talk about names for colors: cinnabar, dusty plum, cypress, coral, ivory, flax, and chamois. Words often gain power as they become more specific. Hunt for specific color names and challenge yourself to find ways to use some of them in your writing.

Vivid Details

Good writers are treasure hunters for vivid, interesting details that will pull the reader inside the experience or inside the writer's thoughts.

One winter day, I was writing with high-school students in Minnesota. I suggested we brainstorm details about winter to get us started with our writing. Snow. Ice. Slushy streets. Warm clothes. Hot cocoa. Snowmobiles. Wind. Mittens. I wrote until we had filled up a white board. Then I stepped back. "How many of these details would someone living in Florida know about winter in Minnesota?"

"None?" someone asked.

"What about television?" I asked. "What about movies—like *Fargo?* You have to find details that will *prove* you are the one who knows what it's like to live through winter here." Some of the details we brainstormed then went into my opening paragraph of *Jakarta Missing.* Have you found details for your scenes that are so vivid and surprising that your reader will be convinced you couldn't possibly have made them up?

Okay. Dad was right. Anyone *would* have to be crazy to want to live through this kind of winter. I know now about days when the hair inside your nose freezes and you feel like someone stuck a toothbrush up there. I know about days when the wind hits you in the face so hard that you gasp for breath and think you must still be asleep and dreaming of Antarctica. The snow squeaks like Styrofoam® when you walk to school, and you can see the breath of every car that passes.

Personality and Voice

Good writers know that a piece of writing—like a person—has a personality.

Characters in fiction each have their own personalities and ways of talking, which is often what readers mean when they talk about a strong sense of *voice* in a novel. Since Dakar is a reader, I could give her a bookish personality. If you want your characters to know certain things or talk in certain ways, pay attention to the books they read and the movies they watch. For example, Dakar got her "allalonestone" from *The Water Babies*, a book the reader of *Jakarta Missing* knows Dakar has read over and over.

And [Tom] swam northward again, day after day, till at last he met the King of the Herrings, with a curry-comb growing out of his nose, and a sprat in his mouth for a cigar, and asked him the way to Shiny Wall; so he bolted his sprat head foremost, and said:

"If I were you, young Gentleman, I should go to the All-alonestone, and ask the last of the Gairfowl. She is of a very ancient clan, very nearly as ancient as my own; and knows a good deal which these modern upstarts don't, as ladies of old houses are likely to do."

Giggles and Grouchy Days: *Do Kangaroos Wear Seat Belts?* and *Rain Romp*

David as a baby

My children were born with a good sense of humor.

They got their funny bones from both sides of our family. My husband's family loves puns, and my father-in-law was making gentle jokes the week he died. My mom's love of language drew her to Scrabble, crossword puzzles, and other word games. She could always be tickled by a good pun.

For a while, my mom, my sisters, and I spent a lot of time trying to top each others' "Tom Swifties." This was a word game named after old-fashioned adventure novels in which hero Tom Swift hardly ever said anything without an adverb tacked on. ("I can do it," he said eagerly.)

To create Tom Swifties, a person has to make some kind of pun with the adverb.

"I forgot to brush my teeth," she said crestfallenly.
"I dried this buffalo meat particularly well," she said jerkily.
"I'm floating!" he said airily.

A LOVE OF FUNNY WORDS AND RIDDLES

When I first started to write books and magazine stories, I had no idea I would end up writing about my own childhood. I thought I was going to write about my children and the things they thought were funny.

My first stories came from listening to my children and jotting down ideas in my idea book. I watched them with their first pet, a kitten that could slip through the shadows and not be seen. As one of them said, "Lots of things could be camouflaged by our cat."

> Yesterday, a cat came to live at our house. The cat is as black as a scare on Halloween night.
>
> When I have to get up in the night, she thinks my feet are mice. She chases them all the way down the hall.
>
> Jeremy doesn't like the cat. "Mommy," he says, "she's sticking me with her pokers."
>
> "She's just trying to play," Mom says.
>
> Jeremy wails like a fire engine. "We need to get a kitty without pokers," he says.

That cat never ended up in a book, although our second one eventually did.

FIRST BOOK

I sent my stories to editors. I got rejection letters.

I wrote more stories. I sent them to editors. I got more rejection letters.

On the occasional days when I opened one of my self-addressed-stamped envelopes (SASE for short) and found an actual letter and not a printed letter, I was thrilled. One of those was from an editor at the publishing house Albert Whitman & Company. She rejected the story I'd sent, but added, "You write very nicely about ordinary happenings, and I hope that someday you can do something that is just right for us."

I sent that editor stories for four years before she accepted one. It became my first published book, *I'm Calling Molly*.

The idea for that book had been planted when David was about four years old and full of admiration for our next-door neighbor, Phaedra.

One day when he ran over to play with her, she was in a bad mood. She crossed her arms and scowled. "I don't know you. I never even saw you before."

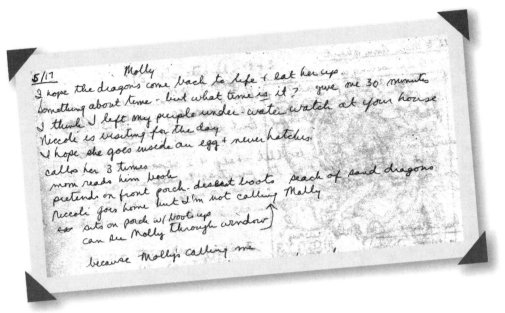

Molly

5/17
I hope the dragons come back to life + eat her up.
Something about time - but what time is it?   give me 30 minutes
I think I left my purple under-water watch at your house
Niccoli is visiting for the day
I hope she goes inside an egg + never hatches.
calls her 3 times
mom reads him book
pretends on front porch. dessert boots   reach of sand dragons
Niccoli goes home but I'm not calling Molly
he sits on porch w/ boots up
can see Molly through window)

because Molly's calling me

From Jane's idea book

Part of me wanted to throttle Phaedra. Part of me admired the way her personality and voice burst through her words. I wrote those words down in my idea book.

About six months later, plot thoughts began to sprout. I jotted them down, too.

Finally, I sat down and wrote the first page.

> My name is Christopher and I live in a house where dragons used to roost under the roof. My best friend's name is Molly, and she lives next door. Molly has hair as red as lava from a volcano. She's the one who told me about the dragons at our house. Molly knows everything about dragons.

I'm Calling Molly was published in 1990. Now, along with my collection of rejection letters, I could start a collection of "attagirls."

SEAT BELTS

That year, we moved from Trinidad, Colorado, to Grand Forks, North Dakota.

I began to get asked to do school visits.

When I wasn't speaking, I continued with my own writing. For a while, I mostly wrote other stories about my children and their lives. Not many of those found their way into publication, but two eventually did.

One was inspired by the days when my three children were still young. For the most part they brushed their teeth when told, and in general minded their parents. But we had big tussles over seat belts. They most emphatically didn't want to wear theirs. Naturally, I insisted. But when I was weary of the tussles, I wished I had a playful book we could read about seat belts.

When I couldn't find a book like that, I tried my own hand at writing a story.

This morning, I was ready to practice hanging from my knees so Jonathan would quit calling me Big Baby. Just then I heard my mom. "Everybody in the car!"

"I'm not going to wear my seat belt," I called back. Nobody answered.

I walked out to the car. "Buckle up," Mom said.

My brothers snapped their seat belts shut. C-c-c-c-click.

I folded my arms. "I'm not going to wear a seat belt ever again."

My older brother reached out and tried to pull me in. "You don't want to get all smashed up if we get in an accident."

"Big Baby," Jonathan said.

Finally, when David was twenty-five and Jonathan was twenty-three, *Do Kangaroos Wear Seat Belts?* was published. Just in time for my *grandbaby* to visit zoos and to not want to wear her seat belt. (More about her later.)

What made an editor finally say yes? First, I came up with the idea of using questions and playful, poetic answers about animals that might wear seat belts. The title then was *Does a Spider Wear a Seat Belt?*

Does a spider wear a seat belt
as it builds its nets with spinnerets
and looping, swooping dashes?
No, a spider's silk is sticky, so a spider never crashes.

Second, I did huge amounts of revision. One editor who was interested in the manuscript asked me to include other safety items and not just seat belts. I thought that made sense. Another suggested I should make the book into a conversation between a specific parent and child and that they have their conversation at the zoo. I thought that made sense, too, even though, sadly, that meant the spider had to go. But I did get to include my favorite African animal, a bush baby.

I was speaking in St. Paul, Minnesota, when I got a note from my editor saying that I was definitely on the right track. "I'm suggesting that you add a little bit more dialogue between the boy and his mother toward the end and add a punch line on page 32," she wrote.

When I have suggestions, my mind goes to work anywhere and everywhere. Tucked in the folder with my editor's note are scribbled bits of *Do Kangaroos Wear Seat Belts?* revisions that I wrote over the next few days on nine pieces of paper.

- An envelope
- Two pages of lined notepaper
- A yellow massage-therapy flyer
- A red Chinese zodiac placemat
- An 8-1/2 by 11 sheet of paper with an email message printed on the back
- A small piece of recycled scrap paper
- A pink Post-it Note®
- A Northwest Airlines boarding pass

In my e-mail mailbox, I have eleven versions of the story saved from that week.

GROUCHY MORNINGS

Revision was also the name of the game for *Rain Romp: Stomping Away a Grouchy Day,* the other picture book that was inspired primarily by one of my children. The book grew out of a gray fall day when I drove my daughter, Rebekah, to school.

Rebekah loved stories. She loved to dress up and act out stories. She loved to read. But she never did like to get out of bed. One overcast morning, she was particularly hostile toward the idea. After driving her to school, I sat down and wrote.

> Gray day.
> Gray grouchy day.
> Mom says, "Yes!"
> I say, "No."
> The sky agrees with me.
> Yesterday, the trees were match tips,
> Blazing red and yellow gold.
> Today, a drizzle
> Like the long slow ripple of
> Grandpa's blues songs
> Soaks the trees,
> Puts out the matches one by one.
> "Why don't you get up?"
> "No."
> "Clean up."

> "No, NO."
> "Wash up? Shape up? Cheer up?"
> Not me
> I'm a
> Howling
> Scowling
> Growling
> Wolverine
> On the prowl.

My editor was attracted to the first lines and the wolverine. She liked the idea of the sky agreeing with the girl telling the story. I could do even more with that, she suggested. Also, I could flesh out the cryptic exchange between the narrator and Mom.

This book, too, took a lot of revision before my editor proclaimed it *just right*. But it became a story almost everyone can connect with. When I ask students how many of them have a hard time getting up in the morning, hands spring into the air. I've signed many copies for people who say what one mother told me: "My daughter is twenty-six years old, but she'll definitely still relate to this story."

Even books inspired by my children have ended up with bits of my childhood in them. I was delighted to include that bush baby in *Do Kangaroos Wear Seat Belts?*

And I was also delighted when I was playing around with a *Rain Romp* revision and realized that of course Dad must croon, "Oh, it's nice to get up in the morning." That's because my siblings and I—and even family friends—have vivid memories of being coaxed, giggling, out of bed by my dad's favorite Scottish song, full of rolling r's: "Oh, it's nice to get up in the morrrning, when the sun begins to shine / At fourr or five or six o'clock in the good old summerrr time."

A sense of humor goes a long way in a children's book, and I was always glad that my children *and* my parents liked to laugh.

WRITERS THINK ABOUT WRITING

Organization
Good writers organize, working hard to find the best structure for a piece and a compelling beginning, middle, and end.

Endings are almost as important as beginnings, and they can be just as challenging, and even discouraging. Every writer knows the feeling of getting well into a story or article, only to realize that he or she has no idea how to end it well. A tried-and-true bit of craft is to look to your beginning.

a) Often in fiction a character grows and changes from the beginning of the story to the end. Look at *Rain Romp* as an example of this kind of ending.

   1) What is the main character's mood at the beginning and at the end?
   2) What is the main character's relationship with her parents at the beginning and at the end?

b) In circular stories, endings tie back into beginnings, creating a kind of circle effect. Look at *Do Kangaroos Wear Seat Belts?* as an example of this kind of ending.

See if you can use either a) or b) to give you an effective ending for a piece you are working on.

> If I was a hippo who
>   wanted to get cool
> Would you grab my hand
> as I was running toward the pool?
> That was great!" said the boy
> I did love the zoo
>   like that
> But I still wish
> I [just]still wish that I cd be a real kangaroo
> When I get big and I'd like to be

Revision notes for *Do Kangaroos Wear Seat Belts?*

Boise
Spokane - cold
Thunder
rumbles +
shakes our
bones.
groan? love you
hug you
silver worms
Rain wiggles +
squiggles like
silver worms
Rain runs down
our necks like
silver worms

stick together
stick it out *romp*
out
work it out *stop*

wandered off
I pull us all under
where
we curl?
a fire warms
~~but~~ set our clothes
pretty soon →

Revision notes for *Rain Romp*

Revising Ideas and Conventions

Good writers revise bravely and boldly, making big changes, and also revise patiently and carefully, making tiny changes.

Look at some of my scribbles from revising *Do Kangaroos Wear Seat Belts?* and *Rain Romp.* Compare my jottings with the finished versions to see where I made big changes and where I changed only a word or two.

Ethiopia at War: My First Novel—*The Storyteller's Beads*

Much of my writing has come from my own experiences in Ethiopia, or my more recent family experiences during my adult life in the United States. Eventually, though, I decided I wanted to write about the current political situation in Ethiopia. The book that resulted was *The Storyteller's Beads.* As I looked toward writing that book I came to realize that I had to know more details about Ethiopia's history in order to understand current events. I would have to do some research. The historical information I located was also very useful when I began to write another book, *Saba: Under the Hyena's Foot* (see Chapter Thirteen). Here is some of the information that might help readers understand the background for *The Storyteller's Beads.*

His Majesty Haile Selassie, the last emperor of Ethiopia, spent many years in the midst of velvet reds and purples, lifting his delicious foods with a heavy silver fork. The keeper of the third door of the emperor's Audience Hall knew how to open the door at the exact right moment, not too soon (which would suggest wanting to hurry the emperor out) or too late (which would cause a stumble in the emperor's dignified step). The bearer of the emperor's pillow knew how to slide it at the precise right instant so as to not leave the royal feet dangling when the emperor was sitting on the throne that had been made for the taller former king. At the Hour of Assignments, those who had permission to approach the emperor kissed his hand and retreated without ever turning their backs, bowing all the way.

One of Emperor Haile Selassie's titles was that of the Lion of Judah. After World War II, a huge lion was carved from black stone and placed near the National Theatre. When the emperor saw it, he said, "Never before have I seen a lion with such a long neck."

Thinking fast, the sculptor replied, "Never before has there been such a great king."

Ethiopia's long age of kings and queens stretched from ancient times (so long ago that there are no records left to study) all the way to 1974, when Emperor Haile Selassie, King of Kings, Lion of Judah, was driven away from his palace in the backseat of a small Volkswagen (usually called a Beetle or Bug). It was the end of the rule of kings in Ethiopia. Haile Selassie's reign came after centuries of rule by kings and emperors and at the conclusion of centuries of resisting colonization.

> One of the most vivid descriptions of Haile Selassie's court is *The Emperor* by Ryszard Kapuscinski (Vintage Books, 1989).

A HISTORY OF RESISTING COLONIZATION

For centuries, Europeans seized African land. In 1588, Portugal had colonies along the African coasts. In the 1650s, Dutch settlers began to claim land in South Africa. It wasn't until the 1880s, though, that the scramble for Africa really began, with Belgium, France, Germany, Great Britain, Italy, Spain, and Turkey claiming chunks of the huge African continent. Early in the history of Ethiopia, Italy was an enemy. By the mid-1800s, Italy was determined to own Ethiopia.

As European powers scrambled, Ethiopia remained an independent kingdom with its own internal fighting. After each Ethiopian emperor died, it took a fearsome struggle to decide who was powerful enough to hold the many parts of the country together, control the lesser kings, and become the king of kings. Because of these power struggles, emperors imprisoned anyone of royal ancestry.

One of those prisoners, Menelik, escaped and built his own army. He was able to become emperor in 1889. The new emperor felt he had two main goals—to bring all of Ethiopia's provinces under control and to watch out for England, France, and Italy, which had colonies surrounding Ethiopia—Italian Somaliland, British Somaliland, French Somaliland, and the Italian colony of Eritrea.

In 1885, King Menelik moved his capital to the present-day capital city of Ethiopia. Queen Taitu, his main adviser, named the new city

Addis Ababa, which means "new flower." Rather than move his capital again when the wood ran out (as trees were cut down for cooking fires and house building), the king had eucalyptus trees imported from Australia. He ordered that priests and other travelers who left the city should be searched to be sure they were carrying seeds out into the countryside so that eucalyptus trees would spread. Soon, the silver blue leaves and sharp smell of eucalyptus were everywhere.

King Menelik loved new things. He was the one who brought the first schools to Ethiopia and the first stamps and the first motorcar. On the other hand, he was annoyed when the Swiss diplomatic adviser took the first photographs of him. "I have been told," he said, "that without my knowledge you made me very small, and stuffed me into a black box, with my whole town, houses, people, and mules. And, what is even more unbelievable, I was standing on my head, with my legs in the air." Once the diplomat explained how cameras of that time worked, the king allowed himself to be photographed a lot—far more than any royal before him.

When he ordered pipes that would bring water into the palace, his advisers were skeptical. Such an idea was going against tradition, against

Addis Ababa, 1997

nature, perhaps even against God. When water came out of the pipe, they were amazed—and they recovered fast. "Such a great king can even cause water to flow uphill," one declared.

In 1896, King Menelik and his troops defeated the Italians who wanted to control Ethiopia. The Ethiopians were the victors at the Battle of Adwa in 1896. It was the first time an African nation had defeated a European nation in war. Ethiopia became the only country to successfully resist Europe's nineteenth-century scramble for Africa. Thus, the king who loved new things ended up saving something very old—the independent kingdom of Ethiopia.

At that time, Italy signed a paper that recognized Ethiopia's independence. But Italy also kept control over the region of East Africa they named Eritrea. And some Italians tucked away feelings of anger and frustration that would one day come bursting out in a terrible act of revenge.

WORLD WAR II AND ITALY'S REVENGE

When King Menelik died, his daughter reigned after him. After King Menelik's daughter died, his cousin, Ras Tefari, was crowned His Imperial Majesty, the Emperor Haile Selassie, Lion of Judah. He used the lion as his symbol, and had real lions living in cages—sometimes the lions even wandered the palace grounds.

Lion on the savanna

When I was growing up in Ethiopia, lions also roamed the flat savanna lands, roaring at night, scaring me in my tent. Every time I saw the emperor's lions, they were behind bars. Even so, they were scary as they rippled from side to side of cages that reeked of raw meat.

The young emperor might have the power of lions, but he soon ran into another kind of power. In 1935, General Benito Mussolini of Italy and his followers were determined to take revenge on Ethiopia for Italy's defeat at the Battle of Adwa in 1896. Italian warplanes roared over the Ethiopian mountains, raining deadly mustard gas onto the people.

The Ethiopian emperor went to the United Nations and pleaded for the world to stand with Ethiopia.

But the world was not yet ready to stand up to the team formed by Germany, Italy, and (later) Japan. The Italian occupation of Ethiopia lasted for five years, during which Ethiopian guerrillas continued to fight in the countryside. A generation of educated Ethiopians was targeted for death in the conflict. Finally, in 1941, Ethiopian fighters, British soldiers, and other troops defeated the Italians and restored the emperor to his throne.

THE END OF THE KINGS

Emperor Haile Selassie ruled for sixty years. During that time, he brought many reforms and advances to Ethiopia. He ordered schools and hospitals and roads built. A law was passed ending slavery. Ethiopia developed a constitution and got a parliament. The Organization of African Unity was established in Addis Ababa, and Ethiopians celebrated their status as the African country that had never been colonized.

But life was hard for the peasants; the people were overtaxed. To feed their families, they overworked the land. Erosion followed. Trees were chopped down for firewood. The black earth cracked, and dust swirled in the air.

After World War II, a United Nations resolution was passed that said Eritrea should govern itself as a region of Ethiopia. But in 1962, Emperor Haile Selassie annexed Eritrea, banning the Eritrean flag and insisting that Amharic be used in offices and schools. For years, Eritrean guerrilla fighters fired guns and hijacked planes and made the roads that led to the Red Sea into places of fear.

In the early 1970s, the northern regions of Ethiopia were hit hard by drought—and since the area had been overfarmed and stripped of trees, it turned into a place of dust and famine. The British Broadcasting Corporation made a film showing that people were starving while the emperor fed bits of food to his favorite lapdog.

Farmers, students, teachers, railway workers, taxi drivers, and soldiers rose up in a giant protest, calling for reform. In June 1974, a group of soldiers, including Major Mengistu Haile Mariam, formed a committee, known by the Amharic word for *committee,* the Dergue. The Dergue brought an end to the time of kings in Ethiopia.

Painting of Mengistu

Many people associated with the emperor were imprisoned, and in September 1974, a small Volkswagen pulled up to the gates of the palace. The once all-powerful emperor ducked his head as he bent down to step into the backseat of the small car and was whisked away to a small house.

Wives and sisters and daughters and children of the most powerful men in Haile Selassie's government were put under house arrest, many of them in the home of Princess Sara, the emperor's daughter-in-law. Many of their sons, brothers, fathers, and friends were executed. Eleven princesses were driven to a prison field, where they sat for four hours. Finally, guards led them through slippery mud into a small, smelly prison cell with no furniture except mattresses. There they stayed for thirteen years, while a Marxist government brought new miseries to many of Ethiopia's people.

WAR, FAMINE, AND ESCAPE

From the mid-1970s until the early 1990s, the period of Dergue rule, the daily lives of people changed enormously. Hundreds of thousands, maybe even millions, of Ethiopians were killed. When people

Beta Israel village

came to claim the bodies of their relatives, they often found flags with the slogan, "Let the Red Terror burn ever brighter."

And the terror did burn bright and hot. Religious persecution seized Orthodox Christians, Protestants, Muslims, and, most particularly, the Beta Israel, Ethiopian Jews.

Hunger and famine ripped apart villages and communities. War with Eritrea blossomed, sweeping almost all of Ethiopia into its devouring mouth. Boys hid in rafters while soldiers ran through houses, scooping up all of the young people they could find and sending them off to be fighters. In Eritrea, airplanes rained bombs, so camps for orphans were built into hillsides. Many people began to live underground.

Hospitals and repair shops also operated underground. "Just roll your tire into the bushes and a new one rolls back," one nurse told a reporter. As the war stretched on, year after year, a whole generation of children in Eritrea grew up underground. Their families waited for cloudy days or until dark to fetch water; pick cabbages, peppers, and papayas; and cook over small fires.

This information was uncovered as being how life was in Ethiopia during the early 1900s, as described in an article titled

> "Eritrea: Region in Rebellion" by Anthony Suau in *National Geographic Magazine,* September 1985. That is where I read descriptions of life in Eritrea and the quote from the nurse.

An African proverb says that when elephants fight, the grass is trampled. As war and hunger raged around them, people began to sneak out of the country. Individuals or families gathered up what they could and began the hard journey over the mountains and through the valleys of the rugged countryside.

People often left at night because the government rarely gave permission for anyone to leave. They traveled for weeks and months, up and down, over the mountains and into the hot deserts of the Sudan, where they could find a bit of safety in refugee camps.

But the camps quickly became overcrowded. Sometimes people couldn't find enough to eat there, either. Many sat in despair, and some even struggled back the way they had come, saying they would rather die at home in Ethiopia, since death seemed inevitable.

Then sometime in the late 1970s or early 1980s, the government of Israel decided to conduct airlifts of the Beta Israel and carry Ethiopian Jews to safety in Israel. Jewish religious leaders and elders had long told

Ethiopian landscape

their people, "We came from the east and some day we will go to the east again and return to Jerusalem." As villagers went about their traditional jobs, making pottery or tending their hot blacksmith fires, whispers ran from one person to the next. *It's time.*

Reporters and other writers had long traveled to Ethiopia to gather information about the Jewish communities there—how the Beta Israel men traditionally were the only Ethiopians to handle and shape metal and what life was like for families and religious leaders. Some of those writers later wrote about the secret details of the adventurers and idealists who dreamed up plans to rescue the Beta Israel from the camps in the Sudan. Others gathered the stories of the survivors who made it to Israel.

While researching my nonfiction book *Ethiopia: Roof of Africa,* I stumbled upon those books. In one—*Operation Moses: The Untold Story of the Secret Exodus of the Falasha Jews from Ethiopia* by Tudor Parfitt (Stein & Day Publishers, 1986)—I found these two sentences: "The guide had gathered fifty other travelers. Among them were a teenaged boy and his sister, a blind girl who would walk all the way to Sudan with a hand on her brother's shoulder."

Those sentences gave me an image of Rahel, the Beta Israel girl in my novel who would walk to the Sudan with her hand on her brother's shoulder. Sahay was born in my imagination when I found an ethnography of the Kemant people. I read that the Kemant thought their Beta Israel neighbors could turn into hyenas at night and cast the "evil eye" upon their enemies—while the ruling Amhara thought the same about the Kemant.

What would happen if I could put a Kemant girl and a Beta Israel girl together on the journey? I wrote my first published novel as a way to answer that question.

Some of my most moving experiences as an author have been the questions and comments sent to me by readers of *The Storyteller's Beads.* A girl in a fifth-grade class in Colorado startled me when she asked, "Did you mean to

Two Ethiopian girls

depress your readers?" But I was comforted by these sentences from a fourth grader in New York City: "I love your book. I think it helps people understand the awful things that happen to people around the world. You have the coolest vocabulary ever."

WRITERS THINK ABOUT WRITING

> ### Organization
> Good writers organize, working hard to find the best structure for a piece and a compelling beginning, middle, and end.

1. The ending of *The Storyteller's Beads* came to me when I read an op-ed piece from the May 29, 1991, edition of the *New York Times*. It described forty jets coming and going from the airport in Israel night and day. The young girls with tattooed patterns on their faces and necks. The old man who knelt and kissed the ground. The cynical reporters watching.

    Then a boy stepped out the door of the plane and lifted a shepherd's flute to his lips. "With his song," *Times* reporter David Grossman wrote, "one live, shimmering spark flew out from under the anvil of our lives. For one whole day, from within the jarring dissonance of our inner sound system, we produced one true note, one clear, harmonious note." If you're stuck in a story, you might want to try writing the ending first.

2. Compare the current beginning of *The Storyteller's Beads* with the beginning I initially used. Why did my editor encourage me to craft a new beginning?

    > The fields were too born that twelfth month, *Nahase*. Usually by this time, the gray-green barley looked to me like light cotton cloth blowing in the mountain winds. Usually the potatoes had flowers and the dark green shoots of the oil seed plants were halfway to my knees. But this year, the year of my sadness, the rains did not fall, and the fields were not wet enough to grow the *tef* grain we use to make our *arah*. Every day when I looked out at the fields, I saw only barley and potato plants curling under the hot sun.

3. Whether you are writing fiction or an introduction to an expository piece, see if you can make your introductory paragraph gripping and active, but also plant details that will give clues about time and place.

Personality and Voice

Good writers know that a piece of writing—like a person—has a personality.

Read the first paragraph of *The Storyteller's Beads*. We often talk about feelings lodging in our hearts, but in Ethiopia emotions lodge in the stomach. List other things in that paragraph that let the reader know Sahay isn't living in the United States in the twenty-first century. It's good practice to write a paragraph or two—or perhaps a journal entry—from the point of view of someone living in another time or place. How can you give your readers clues? What might you need to research before you could do that?

Word Choice

Good writers use words that are specific and interesting, words with sparkle and pizzazz.

As I illustrated in earlier chapters, Ethiopian speech is full of images and proverbs. Find examples of this way of speaking in *The Story-teller's Beads*. Also study my use of italicized words, not only from Amharic but from the Kemant language as well. Can they be figured out from the context? When you check the meanings in the glossary, do you find any surprises? Try sprinkling words from another language into a paragraph of your own and experiment with making the meaning clear from the context.

Finding My Way Back: *Faraway Home* and *Only a Pigeon*

One day, after I finished an author visit, a student slipped this note into my hand: "My explanation on wanting to be a writer. It is my number one choice on my first job. But I really want to be a singer. But a singer won't be coming in a snap."

I laughed to myself ... and thought, *I need to do more to communicate that becoming an author won't be coming in a snap.*

The more I traveled the more I became aware of the many different ways teachers helped young readers connect with my books: research and writing—poems, fiction, informational pieces, reading, art, and drama. There were many ideas and many questions and comments from readers.

"Thank you for telling us about your life. The place you lived was weird, but it was still cool to hear about some place across the ocean."

"I thought *Jakarta Missing* was a great book. You put every word, every sentence, [every] paragraph in the right spot."

"I know how the dad feels in *Faraway Home* because I miss Haiti like you miss Ethiopia."

"Your descriptions are very cool. I love the way the words you use are not-much-used words, like instead of her skin feeling something, it *knows* something."

"Your stories were so funny! I don't think your sister can be as great as you."

"Poetry was boring and tiring to me. Your book *River Friendly, River Wild* opened my eyes and heart."

"I'm sure you must get thousands of fan letters starting this way. But I have to say that I loved your book, *The Storyteller's Beads*. I'm eleven years old, and I could basically be called a bookworm. If I tried to tell you all of the reasons why I enjoyed reading your book, one of three things would happen: my printer would run out of paper before it could finish printing, the envelope I tried to send you this in would burst somewhere on its way to reach you, or, if it somehow made it to you, you would fall asleep around page 1,453."

I got hard questions, too. "Are you going to go back to Ethiopia?" was one that inevitably stabbed my heart because I was positive I would never have the chance. For the longest time, my only connections were with people who had left Ethiopia, often with dramatic stories of escape.

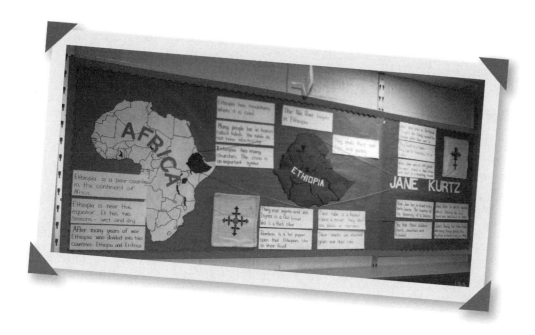

"Do your children like Ethiopia?" was another. It was hard to explain that they had never been out of the United States except for quick visits to Canada. And it was hard to imagine that our family would ever have enough money for five people to travel to Ethiopia. So my children's games and stories were very different from what mine had been as a child.

FARAWAY HOME

One day, my father told me a true story about someone my family had known for a long time. Jerman Disisa grew up near Dembi Dollo, one of the places I visited as a child. He went to a Presbyterian school and eventually was in high-school classes with my friend Sagu, from Maji.

Jerman *(left)* and two classmates

During the years when Mengistu, the harsh dictator of Ethiopia, was encouraging religious persecution, Jerman and Sagu were among those who decided it was time to get out. They wound up in the United States, where Jerman eventually became a professor at a college in South Carolina.

Years later, Jerman showed this picture to his own children, who had always lived in the United States. His son studied the picture and then asked, "Why did you take off your shoes to go to school?"

That, I thought, should be a book. Slowly, I tip-tapped out a paragraph.

Ugh. No good. I deleted it.

I tried again.

Worse. I deleted that one, too.

After the third try went nowhere, I gave up and took a nap. When I woke up, the words poured out.

> When night comes, soft as a curtain falling, Desta's father takes her on his lap. He sings a haunting song with words she doesn't understand.

"My Father's Wild Home." That was the title I gave it. Several years later, after many revisions, it was published as *Faraway Home*. I was like the father in the story, homesick for Ethiopia, trying to help my own children understand my faraway childhood home that included both flamingoes and hyenas.

THE PATH BACK

While I struggled with thoughts and feelings of gulfs and chasms, my parents and some of my siblings gradually began to make their way back to Ethiopia. Chris, my brother, was the first to return, not only to visit but to live.

My two youngest siblings had grown up not in the Ethiopian countryside, as I had, but as city kids. They were only ages five and three when our family moved from Maji to Addis Ababa. Chris went through elementary school and part of high school at Good Shepherd School, but when he was sixteen, our family's life turned upside down as the school closed and my parents decided to return to the United States.

Why didn't your mom and dad retire in Ethiopia? people sometimes ask me.

They certainly intended to.

After I had graduated from college, Mom and Dad were still living and working in Ethiopia, and I managed to get back to visit them several times. I was there for their celebration of twenty years in Ethiopia. But in 1976, increasing religious persecution, roadblocks, shortages, and the government's angry speeches about the U.S. convinced the Presbyterian Church it was time for Americans to leave.

By the late 1980s, shortages and inconveniences were still everywhere. Flour and sugar were hard to buy, and what flour there was tended to be infested with weevils. In the bakeries, cakes and bread were made with half-cornmeal, half-flour. At the one shop that catered to foreigners, shoppers never knew what they would find. A large shipment of Bulgarian jam one week. Pickles the next. For every purchase in that store, a form had to be filled out with five copies made, and since Ethiopians weren't allowed to buy imported goods, buyers had to go through three checkpoints before leaving the store.

But eventually feelings of danger passed, and more adventuresome travelers began not only to visit but to settle and work in Ethiopia. My brother was among them.

Christopher had a family and a teaching certificate by then, and he returned with his wife and two daughters to teach at Ethiopia's first school for girls, a school the Presbyterian church had operated since 1924. He made Ethiopian friends, played basketball on an Armenian team, learned Amharic, and loved almost everything.

Our first collaborative work was on a nonfiction book, *Ethiopia: Roof of Africa* (Macmillan). When I heard that my brother was having adventures taking photographs, I asked if he would like to provide some for my book. He ended up supplying almost all the photos that the editor chose.

When Chris returned, we were at a family reunion in Montana, and I encouraged him to think about using his

Christopher and his basketball team

writing gifts to tell about what he'd seen and experienced. Maybe we should even write a book together. At first, nothing clicked. Then he showed me more of his photos.

One of them made me stare.

The photo was of a boy feeding a baby pigeon. When I asked, he told me that if a mother and father pigeon were killed, their young ones would usually also die. The boys who raised pigeons in Addis Ababa cared for them so tenderly that they chewed up grain and fed the baby pigeons by mouth.

My brother had learned to raise pigeons, too.

Illustration by E.B. Lewis for *Only a Pigeon*. Credit: Reprinted with the permission of Simon & Schuster Books for Young Readers, an imprint of Simon & Schuster Children's Publishing Division from *Only a Pigeon* by Jane Kurtz, illustrated by E.B. Lewis. Illustrations copyright © 1997 by E.B. Lewis.

ONLY A PIGEON

Christopher's pigeon-raising started with a boy named Andualem who used to shine my brother's shoes outside the school's gate. I remembered boys like that. They wanted to shine our shoes—even sneakers could be cleaned and polished. They wanted to sell us gum or candy or tissue. They wanted to watch our car or carry our packages. Anything to make a few coins that would buy a bit of food. "No mother, no father," they often told us.

When I was a teenager, we mostly brushed them away, impatiently. At most, we gave them a slip of paper that would allow them to go to a place that offered free meals for people who had no home except the streets.

My brother now knew Amharic far better than my siblings and I had known the language when we were young. He befriended Andualem, so he got to see what Andualem and his friends did for fun.

They raised pigeons.

I was captivated by the thought of children who had no money for toys or games but still found ways to be play-ful and have something to care for. Who had dreams that lifted their eyes and their hearts. "Do you think you and I could write that story?" I asked.

COLLABORATING AS CO-AUTHORS

Andualem with Hannah Kurtz (the young daughter of Christopher Kurtz)

How to approach it? Chris came to visit, and we haunted the wonderful chil-dren's room at the public library in Grand Forks, North Dakota—my home at that time—lounging in the beanbag chairs and sharing our favorite books. By now, Christopher had returned to the United States and was teaching English as a second language in a school in Portland. I was still reading to my own children and had taken a children's litera-ture course as part of a master's degree in English at the University of North Dakota.

We didn't always agree on the books we loved. One author we did agree on was Cynthia Rylant. The lyrical language she'd used to write a nonfiction book, *Appalachia: The Voices of Sleeping Birds* (Voyager Books, 1998), about the region where she grew up, struck us as the perfect approach for our story.

We read *Appalachia: The Voices of Sleeping Birds* over and over, trying to figure out exactly what wondrous writing secrets Cynthia Rylant knew that we didn't (yet). We turned her into our teacher—by making our-selves students of her writing.

Christopher and I talked about the tone we wanted and the details that were important to include. Then he sat down and typed a section. (He was the one who knew about pigeons and about Andualem's life.) When he was finished, I sat down, read his words, and made everything shorter and tighter, taking out every word that didn't completely earn its keep. He sat down and took another turn, picking and poking.

Baby pigeon

Jane *(back right)* with Andualem *(front left)*, who is holding pages from *Only a Pigeon*

From time to time, I asked him questions. How did the pigeons sound? How did the pigeons smell? He'd never before stopped to consider how a pigeon smelled.

I learned a lot about pigeons. My brother learned a lot about writing. And we both learned that we loved working together. It was hard work but fun.

When we were ready for a break, we walked across the Red River on the ice because Christopher wanted to touch Minnesota. We chased each other and my daughter in circles in a snowy field and laughed so hard that we collapsed into the snow. "My mom doesn't laugh this way," my daughter said.

But with Christopher, I did.

I didn't know it at the time, but one day I'd get to meet Andualem in Ethiopia. If someone had told me I'd have a chance to visit my childhood home, I wouldn't have believed it. I depended on words to paint a picture in the minds of my readers, using my real memories to show what Ethiopia was like. The only way to counter my homesickness, I thought, was to write.

WRITERS THINK ABOUT WRITING

Ideas

Good writers gather ideas that are interesting, focused, and based on things the writer knows about and cares about.

Often, true stories give writers material for interesting pieces. Interview a parent or grandparent or other relative about what things were like when they went to school. How did they travel to school? What did they eat for lunch? What did children do at recess or other breaks? When you're finished, study your notes carefully to see what details jump out at you. Start your writing with something that you found fascinating.

Organization

Good writers organize, working hard to find the best structure for a piece and a compelling beginning, middle, and end.

When crafting a beginning, writers often try to drop the reader right into the middle of the story. Sometimes, though, the opposite approach is needed. Think about a movie that starts out with the camera pulled back to show scenery—to give a strong sense of setting before zooming in to begin the story.

While Chris and I were talking about how to begin *Only a Pigeon,* we decided to pull the camera back. We wanted to show the reader a few important details about Addis Ababa before starting the specific story of one boy's care for his pigeons. Use *Only A Pigeon* as a mentor text to help you experiment with that kind of introduction.

Rhythm and Beat

Good writers listen to the rhythms of sentences and pay attention to how one sentence flows into and fits with the next.

The way the first words of *Only a Pigeon* are arranged on the page gives the reader a good clue about how to read a very long sentence aloud. Count how many words are in that first sentence. Use it as a model for a long sentence of your own.

Peeking into History—*Saba: Under the Hyena's Foot*

Ethiopia is home to a few of the oldest stories on the earth.

One Ethiopian woman plays a heroic part in a traditional story that is still told through paintings, a story that was at the heart of the Ethiopian monarchy. For many years the story of the Queen of Saba (Sheba) and her visit to King Solomon was told. In the fourteenth century it was written into the *Kebre Negast, The Glory of Kings*, which also records that the queen and King Solomon had a son, named Menelik. When the boy was old enough, he visited his father to learn the laws of Israel—and when the time came to depart, he couldn't bear to leave behind the Ark of the Covenant. So he slipped it away with him, carrying it back to Ethiopia.

THE QUEEN OF SHEBA, KING SOLOMON, AND THE ARK OF THE COVENANT

A story has power to give a country its identity. Every Ethiopian king from the fourteenth century on claimed to be descended from King Solomon and the Queen of Sheba. Some historians think the Ethiopian Jews—or Beta Israel—arrived with Menelik. Some also think that the Ark of the Covenant may well be hidden to this day in Axum, now a small town in northern Ethiopia. The ark has long played a big role in the life of the Ethiopian Orthodox Christian church.

POWER STRUGGLES IN ANCIENT CITIES

Christianity's appearance in Ethiopia is extremely old. According to tradition, it was when two Syrian Christian boys were shipwrecked on the Red Sea and taken into the king's court where they tutored the king's sons in many things including their religious beliefs. King Ezana then declared Orthodox Christianity to be the state religion. Coins with crosses on them have been dug up and dated to the king's reign. Massive churches were sculpted out of rock. Lalibela is a site of those ancient and elaborate carvings and paintings in the churches. They are often described as one of the wonders of the world.

Islam, the other religion that shaped Ethiopia, first came through a gesture of peace. A king of Ethiopia offered safety to some of the family members of the Prophet Mohammed who were being persecuted. In the fifteenth century, though, an Islamic warrior named Ahmed Gran led a fierce sweep through Ethiopia, burning churches and monasteries. Much of Ethiopia was under Islamic control from 1529 to 1543. The Ethiopian king appealed to Portugal, and Christopher

Lalibela church carved into a cliff from the top down

da Gama, son of the explorer Vasco da Gama, was sent with 400 men. In the end, Ahmed Gran was defeated, but the city of Harar remained a strong center of Islamic life and trade.

Portuguese advisers may also have helped design or encourage the building of castles that turned the city of Gondar into the next center of power. In the late 1500s, the king's court shifted from place to place, moving once wood and other natural resources were used up. Emperor Fasilades established a permanent capital in Gondar when he built the first of his castles in 1635.

During the first years of my life in Ethiopia, I didn't know anything about Axum, Gondar, Harar, or Lalibela. Since I grew up in the southwest corner of Ethiopia and studied American history while I was in school, those historic places weren't part of my life. But one year, my mom and dad decided we would take a vacation and drive north.

The palace of King Fasilades at Gondar

Our most startling and almost scary stop was the Blue Nile waterfall called *Tis Issat*, which means "Smoke of Fire." I watched the water thunder down and crash onto the rocks, sending droplets bouncing into the air in a fine, thick mist that looked like smoke.

But, oh, the castles of Gondar! I didn't yet know the stories of the emperors who built these walls and turrets and curving stair-cases. I hadn't read the writings of historians, who describe walls "decorated with ivory, mirrors and paintings of palm trees, its ceiling covered with gold-leaf and precious stones." As I looked around, though, I knew fascinating things must have happened there. And I was right.

City of Gondar today

In the early 1990s, when I was working on my first major picture book, *Fire on the Mountain,* I included Gondar, and E.B. Lewis created a painting of the ruined castles. I put Gondar in my first published novel, *The Storyteller's Beads.* In 1997, I actually got to see Gondar again.

When I was invited to Ethiopia to speak in three international schools, they offered me a trip, and I chose to see the rock churches of Lalibela, something I'd never seen, and Gondar, that mysterious city that loomed so large in my memory.

This time, I asked more questions. I took more pictures. And I thought, *I want to write about this some day.*

WRITING HISTORY WITH SABA (SHEBA)

My opportunity came in 2002. I was contacted by an editor at Pleasant Company, the creator of the American Girl books and dolls, about a series called "Girls of Many Lands." They wanted one of the three new books to be set in Africa.

When Rebekah was about ten, she read every American Girl book, begged for a doll, and acted out plays. I knew if anyone had a chance to interest readers in girls' lives around the world, it would be Pleasant Company. Also, I'd heard from two other authors of books in the series—Mary Casanova and Laurence Yep—that Pleasant Company cared deeply about getting the historical details right.

Each book in the series also had a doll, and the production people were thinking of a Masai girl because they were drawn to a doll wearing a gorgeous, colorful, multi-strand bead necklace. Unfortunately for me, the Masai live in Kenya. "Isn't there any way we can move the story across the border into Ethiopia?" I asked.

Rebekah mixing dolls and history

My editor became a strong advocate. I told her that the world already had books about small houses and wild animals of Africa, and I wanted to write about castles. She convinced the production people that Ethiopia was the right African country for the Girls of Many Lands series. The result was *Saba: Under the Hyena's Foot*.

The editor told me I could choose any time period. Then she asked a vital question: When did girls start wearing the clothing that's become traditional in Ethiopia today? What kind of documentation could I find that would answer that question?

Historical fiction is a demanding genre, as an editor once pointed out, because it has to be good fiction and it has to be good history. I decided my story would start in an isolated part of northern Ethiopia with a girl and her brother who have been sheltered from their past. To write those rural scenes, I was able to use many of my real memories.

Jane in front of her first house in Maji

I decided that Saba and her brother would then be kidnapped and carried off to Gondar. For those scenes, I needed details that weren't part of my memories.

An Icelandic proverb says, "Keen is the eye of the visitor." It was visitors to Ethiopia, writing about the things that puzzled and delighted and astonished them there, who would give me most of the material I needed. Many recorded what they saw, touched, smelled, tasted, and heard, including a huge drum that was thumped forty-four times, giving the people time to gather when a nobleman wanted to make a proclamation. By the time the last boom faded away, people had to be standing in front of the man and ready to listen.

I had to rummage for months before I found someone who had written about what girls in Ethiopia wore in earlier times. But alas for me, I discovered that I wasn't going to be able to seat my princess a little to the left of the emperor on his golden stool at a table groaning with food, or in an alcove gazing up at delicate stars painted on plates of ivory. She wasn't going to get to watch the king's mule trotting on the Persian rug because the earliest time I could say for sure what girls wore was the mid-1800s, and by then, Gondar was in turmoil.

As one Ethiopian scribe wrote, the royal city was now weak, like a worthless flower that children picked in the rainy season. The kings didn't have their old powers, and warriors deposed one ruler, put another on the throne, then restored the first, and so on. At one point, six emperors were alive at the same time—and some had been deposed and restored several times in their lifetimes.

I had to make detailed, complicated notes just to clarify in my own mind who was on the throne during which years (or months), and who the vital players were in the year I chose, 1846. This was just before Gondar collapsed.

Fortunately, every era has its fascinating historical figures.

I discovered a strong queen who was described by one European traveler this way: "Greedy, miserly, clever, violent, ambitious, despotic, vain, coquettish, she stopped at nothing." Another real person who went into the pages of my book was Ras Ali, head of the noblemen. He came out of the powerful Oromo community. Some mistrusted him because they said he might claim to be a Christian but he still had an Islamic heart.

And then there was Kassa. The *ras*, or general, and the empress wanted him on their side and coaxed him there by offer-

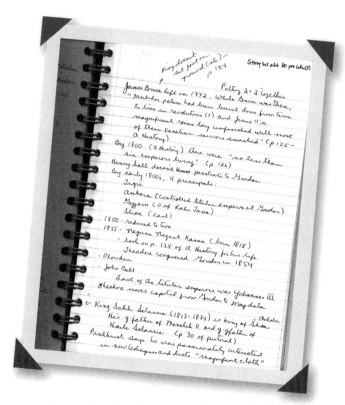

A page from Jane's notes as she researched the history of Gondar

ing Ras Ali's daughter in marriage. They were joined by something that was a big part of my childhood: hyenas. To this day, Addis Ababa has almost no trash collection, so as dusk gathers, hyenas stream out of the

Hyenas on the African savanna

hills and into the city streets. I used to hear their odd whooping as I lay in my bed. According to visitors to Gondar, hyenas made it dangerous to go out after dark then, too.

I had put hyenas in *Fire on the Mountain,* but only in one sentence. Now I had the chance to turn those scary animals into real characters, sources of tension and danger, a role they played in real life in Ethiopia in the 1840s and a role they still play to this day.

WRITERS THINK ABOUT WRITING

Revising Ideas and Conventions

Good writers revise bravely and boldly, making big changes, and also revise patiently and carefully, making tiny changes.

After I finished my first polished draft of *Saba,* I had a phone conversation with the editor, during which I jotted down these notes: Really liked this character—sweet. I want to know what she wants. Can you bring that out sooner? Why is she so fearful? Does her grandmother tell her stories of bad people? Do people ever come by? Is it important that Saba and her brother be isolated? If so, why?

Next time you revise a story, ask yourself whether the reader knows what your main character wants. How early did you show it? How did you show it? Have someone read your story and ask you the kinds of questions my editor asked me. You may well find that those questions will help you make your writing stronger and clearer.

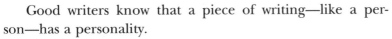

Personality and Voice

Good writers know that a piece of writing—like a person—has a personality.

In fiction, a writer's voice often shines through his or her characters' voices. A writer's job is to create people who are not "generic," but instead people who are distinctive in the ways they talk and move and fight and play. When I was finding ways to give Saba her voice, I drew on the Ethiopian love of clever sayings.

Some experts think that Amharic started as a secret language, which might explain why so many Ethiopians consider it clumsy and even offensive to speak boldly, bluntly, and directly. Traditionally, Ethiopian children were raised to avoid revealing too much of what they were thinking and feeling lest they give others too much power. This approach to language leads to thousands of interesting proverbs that constantly find their way into conversations.

It is better to let your feet to slip than your tongue.
If you hide your disease, you can't expect to be healed.
Some situations can be like the cow that gave birth to fire—she can't lick it or her tongue will burn, but she can't ignore it because it's her child.
Loose teeth will not stop aching until they are rooted out.
Telling a secret to the wrong person is like pouring grain into a torn bag.
After the month of Maskram there are no rains, just as after the rooster crows, there is no night.

Make a collection of proverbs using books or by interviewing family members or school personnel. Use *Saba* as a mentor text to show you how a character can speak in proverbs.

Organization

Good writers organize, working hard to find the best structure for a piece and a compelling beginning, middle, and end.

Often students ask me if I will write a sequel to *Saba* because some threads are left dangling at the end of the story—but nevertheless my editor liked my ending because it did show that Saba had grown and changed. Often, a writer uses a character's thoughts, feelings, and/or actions at the end of a story to show (not tell) this change. Study how I did this in *Saba*. Consider how you might use a defining action or a character's thoughts or feelings to end your story effectively.

Disaster! *River Friendly, River Wild*

It took me several years to write and then revise *The Storyteller's Beads*. Month after month, I put my imagination to work, trying to see vividly what it would be like to leave home with only a few hours' notice, perhaps never to return. While I worked to put myself into my characters' heads and hearts, I had no idea that soon I was going to experience the real thing myself. It changed my book—and my own heart.

Jane at International School in Addis Ababa

I was thinking about my novel in late March 1997, when I flew out of Addis Ababa to Frankfurt, Germany, and headed home to Grand Forks, North Dakota. As I stepped off the plane, I thought, *How strange to have just been in a place bursting with sound and color and spicy smells, and now to be in a place so gray and white.* Although it was spring, no bits of green were showing.

The winter brought more snow to Grand Forks than any year since our family arrived in 1990. Piles of snow filled the streets and yards. Neighbors helped one another clear sidewalks and driveways.

FLOOD

Early in April I traveled to Massachusetts to speak at a school. On my return trip I got as far as the Minneapolis airport, but no planes were flying into Grand Forks. A blizzard had covered power lines with ice, pulling them down, and the airport had no electricity. Airport officials hoped to restore it soon. Until then, no flights could land. For four days I waited. Each day I was told that flights were scheduled to depart again. Each day the flights came up cancelled, cancelled, cancelled.

Finally flights resumed, and I arrived home to the news that the Red River was rising. The Red River ran right through our neighborhood. The year before, the river had risen and threatened to go over the dikes, but the danger then was nothing like what was to come this particular year.

On my birthday, April 17, I woke up to the scratching sounds of bags being filled with sand. People were piling them around the house across the street. I looked over everything for my school visit in Grand Forks, which was coming up the next day. Then I went to the dentist.

At the dentist's office I was told I had a cracked tooth. I

David in the snowy backyard

Sandbags piled in front of the house across the street

made an appointment to have it pulled in a few days and headed home. When I walked into our front hall, I saw file cabinets, boxes of photographs, pillows and bedding, dresser drawers full of clothes, and other things jammed into the living room.

My daughter ran to tell me that water was leaking through one of the dikes. The city was suggesting evacuation of our neighborhood. Her best friend's parents had come over and helped to move almost everything out of the lower level of our home.

Our house was on the highest ground of any in that neighborhood. For any flooding to disturb us, it would first have to devastate the hundreds of houses where Lincoln Drive sloped down toward the river. That seemed unthinkable. "Surely they don't mean that *we* should evacuate," I said.

My husband thought we should go. Just in case.

Feeling silly, I had the kids each pack an overnight bag. "Take your baseball and gloves," I told my sons, "so you'll have something to do." I packed my school speaking supplies for the next day, and we put everything in the car for the drive to another Grand Forks neighborhood, where our friends the Johnsons had invited us to stay in their house. "Let's go," my husband called.

What about the cat?

Rebekah with Figaro

"We're only going to be gone a couple of days," I said. "Put out plenty of food and water. She'll be fine here."

But my daughter, Rebekah, couldn't remember a time when Figaro didn't live with us. The cat had to come.

The Johnsons had a cat, Kiwi, and the two might not get along. It would only be a few days. But after a long discussion, I sighed, gave up, packed the litter box and food, and drove to the Johnsons' house with apologies.

That evening, my husband went out to find a

birthday cake and came back reporting that water was too high around our house to get in without wading boots. He'd turned on the pump in the basement. I talked on the telephone with the editor working on *The Storyteller's Beads*. She said the book was coming along beautifully. She'd just sent me revision notes—I should get them by the next day.

In the background, the cats hissed.

The next day, school was cancelled and we spent the day sandbagging. Television and radio reports crackled with speculation about the impending flood. Over supper, we made jokes about the strange situation. Someone said we should probably sleep with our bags packed. We laughed, but at four in the morning, I awoke to someone knocking.

Everybody out.

Later, we learned the whole story. When ice floes jammed against the bridge over the Red River, the water had nowhere to go but outward—over the dikes. Since Grand Forks is so flat, eventually 80 percent of the city had to evacuate. Near the river, water swelled to the roofs of houses. In other places, it touched the bottom of street signs. And houses on high ground got exactly what we'd joked about: basements full of water.

SURVIVAL

That night, our family drove through the darkness toward a temporary shelter at the nearby Air Force base, but I dozed off, and my husband decided to head on north to the little town where he'd been working. While we waited for daylight, we slept in the basement of the local Presbyterian church. By the next day, we were depending on the kindness of strangers.

After that, news of what was happening came from television. In Grand Forks, fire blossomed in a downtown building that sat on a flooded city street. Helicopters chop-chop-chopped over the city, dropping buckets of water. On the television screen we saw boats navigating up and down the streets. Some of them carried pet rescue people going from house to house to try to save animals. As we watched a dripping, clawing cat being forced into a bag, I smoothed Figaro's fur, thinking about how close we had come to leaving her behind.

Now I knew firsthand what it was like to make plans and walk calmly along, only to have the well-known path drop away.

Tough to live through.

Great for my novel revision.

The Red River flood of 1997 taught me the emotions of upheaval and also about survivor guilt, things I used in *The Storyteller's Beads*. It also reminded me that though I couldn't stop the flood from wiping away one great neighborhood, the flood couldn't stop my scribbling pen or tapping computer keys.

Six weeks later, I sat on the front porch of my house watching big machines scoop up the garbage. I took out my notebook and wrote about it.

> Down the street, the little square machine scooches along and picks up refrigerators and stoves.
>
> The big machine with a long neck lumbers and swings, nudges garbage into the street and picks it up in its teeth.
>
> On Belmont Road, a huge yellow machine bends its neck and gobbles the old clay of the temporary dike.
>
> Stop
> Working
> They all beep beep beep with a high, yellow sound.

Lincoln Park neighborhood after the flood

When I showed some of the poems I'd written to my Simon & Schuster editor, she said if I could turn the poems into a story, she'd like to publish it. Before that could happen, I had two big writer's jobs ahead of me. The first was to ask myself which of my poems absolutely had to be in. Here is one that came out:

QUILT RESCUE
Two great-grandma quilts sit
side by side
draped over sawhorses on the lawn.
The great-grandma I never met
made the one on the left.
I've gone to sleep at night
touching the threads her fingers sewed,
the squares her fingers chose,
and the designs she dreamed.
Mom says the quilts were soaked,
but maybe mud didn't get in.
We take them to the Laundromat,
wash them twice in cold water
and once with soap.
They tumble dry.
I scoop them up and wrinkle my nose.

Ugh.
I don't love the smell of river water
anymore.

The second thing I had to think about was that stories need tension. Something must keep readers turning the pages. When I was brainstorming with a group of writers, someone asked the big question. *What if?*

What if we had left the cat behind?

The question brought back memories of those television pictures. The pet rescues. I sat down to revise, naming the left-behind cat in my story Kiwi—in honor of the Johnsons' cat, which had to put up with a guest kitty.

When I talk about this story, someone almost always asks, "What happened to the cat?" Any element that makes the reader wonder *What happens next?* is good for tension.

By September 1997, my family was living in a Federal Emergency Management Agency (FEMA) trailer. We learned how hot trailer walls become in the summer and what it was like when so much ice built up in the winter that the door wouldn't close. Through it all, I kept writing: *The Storyteller's Beads, Rain Romp,* and the book of poems written after the flood, *River Friendly, River Wild.* "Never think you have to wait for ideal circumstances before you plant yourself in the chair," I tell writers.

In 2000, *River Friendly, River Wild* won the Golden Kite award from the Society of Children's Book Writers and Illustrators for the best picture-book text of the year. I had the pleasure of standing at the Society's Los Angeles conference in front of 1,000 people. Friends held up a quilt made by my writer friends, a quilt that provided comfort and warmth in the days after the flood.

I still miss the Lincoln Drive neighborhood—now a park—and the things I lost in the flood. Every Christmas, it's hard to drag out the few things that were saved from the Christmas box, hard to want to decorate with anything new.

But, somehow, having written about it helps. And since *River Friendly, River Wild* has been out in the world, I've had the pleasure of knowing that some readers came to sense a little of what surviving a flood is really like. In Chicago, a boy came up during my author visit and said, "My teacher told me not to tell you this ... but she cried when she read your book to us."

Actually, it was a perfect thing to tell me.

Knowing that my book had built a bridge from my life to that of the teacher and her students made my sadness retreat into its own little corner at least for an hour. At least for a day.

WRITERS THINK ABOUT WRITING

Revising Ideas and Conventions

Good writers revise bravely and boldly, making big changes, and also revise patiently and carefully, making tiny changes.

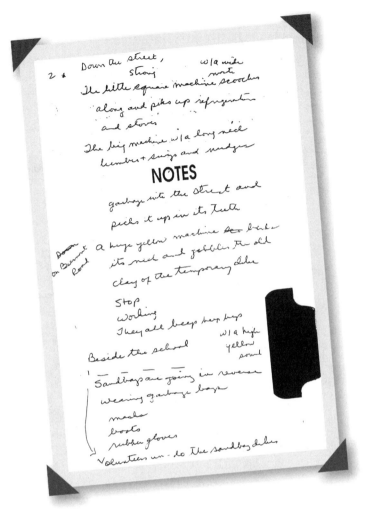

River Friendly, River Wild began as scribbled words on notebook pages. My big revision work was shaping the story, deciding what to put in and what to leave out, finding my tension line and keeping it taut from the beginning to (almost) the end.

Later, I needed to do small, meticulous revisions. I had written that the days were now "warm as toast popped from a toaster." My editor reminded me that "warm as toast" had probably been overused and challenged me to come up with a new simile.

The line "wrist twist 'til the bag's closed" didn't come until I was polishing. Although I wrote plenty of rhyming poetry, I always advise young poets to stay away from rhyme. That's because I think it's important to explore other ways of playing with words, and also because using rhyme often keeps a poet from thinking about what he or she really wants to say. But you can try internal rhyme without having to commit to having a rhyme at the end of every line. Use *River Friendly, River Wild* as a mentor text to help you see how.

Personality and Voice

Good writers know that a piece of writing—like a person— has a personality.

In the poem "Mad," the narrator says people tell her she should consider herself lucky, but she doesn't feel lucky. Readers have told me, "That's just how I felt." As someone once commented, "Writers say what other people only think." Part of voice is daring to be honest. Use "Mad" as a mentor text for writing a short piece about one of your small moments of strong emotion.

Sparkling Words

Good writers use words that are specific and interesting, words with sparkle and pizzazz.

When I was in the second grade, my teacher wrote on my report card, "We have enjoyed Jane's poems. They are exceptionally good for her age. Perhaps it is one of her talents."

Although I can't remember those poems, I have copies of others from when I was young. All of my poems rhyme—so I assume my second-grade poems did, too.

Whether you are writing poetry or prose, let go of rhyme but do practice other ways of playing with words. You can see examples of alliteration, assonance, and other playful elements in *River Friendly, River Wild*. Try those out in your own writing.

Rhythm and Beat

Good writers listen to the rhythms of sentences and pay attention to how one sentence flows into and fits with the next.

Usually, repetition is one thing that makes a piece of writing boring. But sometimes writers use repetition on purpose. When I wrote the poem, "Sandbagging – April 12," I was trying to capture the ways we did the same actions over and over and over. Study what I did in the poem and then see if repetition of a word, phrase, or sentence—clearly done on purpose—can add a special rhythm to a piece of writing. (Hint: To make sure the reader knows you've repeated on purpose, it's often better to use a clear, unusual word or phrase to repeat.)

Playing Fair: *Bicycle Madness*

One year, I began to write about a reformer who lived in the late nineteenth century and believed life in the United States could be fairer. It was a photograph that introduced me to Frances Willard. But there were two things that made me like her so much that I wanted to write about her. The first was her passion for and belief in fairness. The other was the way she ran and jumped fences and built a tree house and climbed onto stumps to give speeches when she was a girl—and the fact that she cried when she turned sixteen and had to put on long skirts and pin up her hair.

I stumbled upon the photograph when I was living in Trinidad, Colorado. At the time, I was doing research about the turn of the century, when southern Colorado boomed. Trinidad, Colorado, in those days was a swirling, swinging town that people came flocking to from all over the world. In the late 1800s, coal was so valuable it was often called "black gold." And southern Colorado—with its rich veins of coal—was wide open for miners.

So I read about coal, about Mother Jones (that feisty woman who walked at the front of marches for miners' rights), and about children working in factories. I turned the page and saw a photograph of a woman balanced on a bicycle. Her skirts were down to her ankles. Three men in top hats seemed to be holding onto the bicycle with a certain amount of desperation. The woman was looking ahead with an interesting expression. Grim determination? Panic?

Who was this person, and what was she doing?

Illustration from *Bicycle Madness* based on the photograph. Credit: Book cover and interior art illustrated by Beth Peck from *Bicycle Madness*. Illustrations © 2003 by Beth Peck. Reprinted by permission of Henry Holt and Company, LLC.

FRANCES WILLARD'S BICYCLE

Curiosity is a good thing for a writer. There was only a brief caption under the photograph. That's where I first read the name *Frances Willard*. But I was sitting in a library, after all, and it didn't take long to find out that there was much written by and about her. In fact, to my surprise, I discovered that at one time she was the most famous woman in the whole United States.

I decided historical fiction was the best way to tell the story I wanted to tell. I loved the nonfiction aspect, though, so I decided to put as many of Frances Willard's real words into her mouth as I possibly could. I *had* a lot of her words available. And I didn't want to fall into the trap of creating a modern character and plopping her into the past, the way writers sometimes do with historical fiction.

At the turn of the century, Frances Willard and other reformers (including the suffragettes Susan B. Anthony and Elizabeth Cady Stanton) were determined to speak out about the deep unfairness of life in the United States. For the children working in factories who had no chance to go to school. For the men who took all of the family money (at the time most women didn't earn any money for themselves) and spent it in saloons. And for the women, who couldn't vote.

Frances Willard had her schoolmarmish side. She had been the dean of women at Northwestern University, and she could shake her finger at an out-of-line person with the best of them. In this way, she reminded me a little of my own grandmother, who didn't have patience for behavior she considered unworthy of a person's best.

But Frances Willard wasn't a stuffy person. Her pets included a big, silky cat with a curling tail—who jumped to her side when she spoke and who wore a bib and ate at the table. She climbed an Egyptian pyramid and clung there with the wind howling around her. All her life, as she wrote in several autobiographical works, she drew on her memories of her childhood, when she and her brother and sister made sleds, took care of dozens of pets, set traps for quails, and "played 'Fort City' with great zest."

It was these childhood romps she was thinking about—even though she was in her fifties—when she decided to learn to ride a bicycle.

BLOOMERS

From the invention of early bicycles, some women wanted to ride. This was true even when bicycles had a gigantic front wheel, and riders were instructed, "It is an excellent thing for a beginner to *learn to fall properly,* and without injury to either himself or the wheel." But in the late 1800s a much safer bicycle (nicknamed the "ordinary") was built, and a craze for riding followed.

Not everyone approved. Some thought the new machines were harmful. Women and children in particular were told to beware. Children might damage their nervous systems. One doctor warned about "bicycle hands," that started with a little numbness and could lead to crumpled hands that couldn't hold anything and were completely useless. A newspaper reported that "bicycle gums" could come from riding too fast and heating up the system. Another doctor diagnosed "bicycle eye." It supposedly was caused by bicycle riders who studied the ground and then lifted their gaze to look ahead.

Then there was "bicycle twitch." Actually, bicycle twitch was a joke, a condition that supposedly came from women who made quick twists to look back and ask, "Are my bloomers in place?"

Bloomers had been invented in the mid-1800s by women who wanted more comfortable clothing for such exertions as walking on the Oregon Trail. Magazine and newspaper cartoons had a great time mocking the costume, with drawings of women looking extremely silly. Bloomers disappeared under what one writer calls an "avalanche of ridicule."

Jane with Frances Willard's bicycle

But with huge numbers of women wanting to ride bicycles, bloomers came storming back into fashion. In June 1895, the *Chicago Tribune* ran a little ditty that started this way:

"Sing a song of bloomers out for a ride,
With four and twenty bad boys running at her side."

Bicycle riding changed women's clothing. And it encouraged women to think of themselves as independent and strong.

That's why Frances Willard wanted to learn how to ride. She had powerful feelings about her active childhood in Wisconsin. "Our coasting down the hill was wonderful to see," she wrote. "Our fishing with a crooked pin, small bait and less fish, in the mellow-voiced river; our climbing trees for toothsome hickory nuts, beating the bush for mealy hazel-nuts, and scouring the pastures for sweet-smelling plums that grew wild; our play-houses with dishes moulded from clay in my 'china manufactory,' and dolls for which I declined to make clothes."

She thought that maybe, on the seat of a bicycle, she could feel those same joyous, free sensations. Eventually, she wrote an entire book, called *A Wheel Within a Wheel*, about what it was like learning to ride a bicycle. It includes the time she took a spill and decided she should give up on the whole idea.

Lillie, the character I made up to be Frances Willard's next-door neighbor, also sprang out of my memories and experiences. As an avid

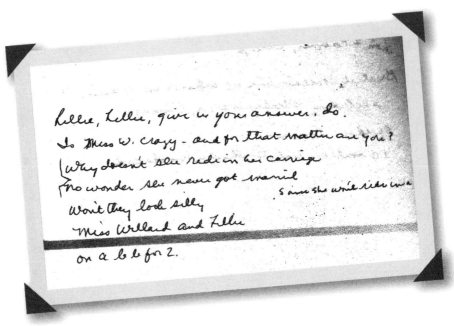

Jane's rough notes for *Bicycle Madness*

reader, I had always been a pretty good speller. But I did remember what it was like quizzing my son David on his spelling words, starting when he was in the third grade. I also remembered what it was like to arrive at boarding school and find that some of my roommates had been at Good Shepherd School the year before and were already fast friends. How painful it was to wonder whether a friend I adored would leave me the next month and go skipping off with someone else. How much it hurt when other students found something to mock me about.

A song that I used to sing when I was a child—"The Bicycle Built for Two"—gave me an idea for how Lillie's friends and enemies would taunt her. I still remembered every word. I quickly took out my idea book and began to scribble my own version.

It took a great deal of research to be able to write historical fiction about something that happened in the 1880s, but I was able to go to Evanston, Illinois, to visit Frances Willard's house, now a museum. Walking around, looking at her photographs and all the things that belonged to her, I was able to gather the details I needed for the house and the neighborhood.

I researched hundreds of different things, from slang words of the time, to what children were commonly named, to the games, such as marbles, that they played every day. Of course I'd heard of *Webster's Dictionary*, so it was fun to look at the little book Lillie held in her hands when she wanted to study her spelling words. The president of Yale College was determined to name it "A Grammatical Institute of the English Language: Part I." It came to be commonly called "Webster's Blue-Backed Speller."

In 1880, the publisher said in an interview that Webster's Speller "has the largest sale of any book in the world except the Bible. We sell a million copies a year." Many years later, I opened one, myself, and read through the words.

> The American Spelling Book
> Containing
> The rudiments
> Of the
> English language
> For
> The use of schools
> In the
> United States
> By Noah Webster, Esq.

Unless time travel becomes real someday, we will never be able to experience what life was really like for the millions of people who came before us. When I read historical fiction that has been well researched, though, I feel as if I am being tugged back, zooming through time to stand on the brick streets, perhaps with someone who was once as famous as Frances Willard.

Meanwhile, some threads come snaking forward through time to tie our lives to theirs in other ways. Every time I vote, I remember that women risked harm and ridicule because they thought I should have a voice. Every time I find a way to stand up for fairness, I know I'm stepping in the shoes of many Americans who came before me, including my own father and grandfather.

WRITERS THINK ABOUT WRITING

Personality and Voice
Good writers know that a piece of writing—like a person—has a personality.

1. One of the goals a writer has when writing dialogue is for the reader to know who is speaking even without the tag ("Lillie said," for example). If a writer has done a great job of hearing a character's voice, each person in the story should speak differently. Copy some lines of dialogue spoken by Lillie, by her brother, and by Frances Willard in *Bicycle Madness*. See whether a classmate can tell who is speaking. Now try the same strategy with one of your own stories.

2. When you are writing nonfiction about people, places, or events, it will add strength if the reader can hear a person speaking. Often, however, a writer is tempted to have "generic" dialogue—that is, dialogue that sounds as if anybody could have said it. Carefully consider how the people in your life talk. What are their favorite expressions? How do they express anger? Delight? If you don't know, start listening. Take notes. Become a sleuth in the tradition of Harriet from *Harriet the Spy*.

Interesting Ideas
Good writers gather ideas that are interesting, focused, and based on things the writer knows about and cares about.

The idea for *Bicycle Madness* would never have come to me if I hadn't seen a photograph. Perhaps with help from your friends and/or classmates, gather a shoebox full of interesting pictures. Pull one out. Jot down five sense details that pop into your mind as you study it. Write character descriptions of the people in your picture. Try one-line captions. See if any of the pictures will help you think of something you want to write about.

Vivid Details

Good writers are treasure hunters for vivid, interesting details that will pull the reader inside the experience or inside the writer's thoughts.

When describing a scene or something in it, writers sometimes add the wrong kinds of details. If a writer wants to describe a person's appearance, for example, there are hundreds of choices: hair color, clothing, eye color, shoes, height, weight, or bland adjectives such as "nice" or "weird" or "funny."

One better possibility is to paint a word picture. Look at the way Frances Willard described Gladys as a horse. Mark Twain wrote in a similar way about his bicycle. "Mine was not a full-grown bicycle," he wrote, "but only a colt—a fifty-inch, with the pedals shortened up to forty-eight—and skittish, like any other colt." Try this technique to describe a person or thing in a piece of writing you are working on.

Giving Voice to Stories: *In the Small, Small Night*

I often speak at schools and at conferences for fellow educators. I meet many wonderful people and, as is common, one experience often leads to another.

After a presentation at the International Reading Association in San Diego, some teachers thought I might like to speak at a reading conference in Bahrain. Soon I had an invitation to speak not only at the conference but also in five schools in the Persian Gulf, a part of the world I never thought I'd visit. It embarrasses me to admit that, up until that time, when I heard the words "Persian Gulf," I thought only about war and sorrow.

The countries I visited were full of tall buildings and modern, bustling life. The part of the gulf I walked beside was idyllic. In Oman, I left my shoes lying in the sand while my husband and I strolled with the librarian's two daughters, picking up shells. When we returned, just as we'd been assured, the shoes were still there.

In Kuwait, Oman, and Abu Dhabi, children asked me, "Are you going to write about us?"

"I never know for sure what I'll end up feeling compelled to write about," I told them.

Most of the visits I have made to international schools have introduced me to many interesting students. Some of the students I've met—even second and third graders—have lived in more countries than I had even visited when I was their age. And again and again I see that writing has power. Sometimes complex realities need just the right novel or short story or movie or memoir to illuminate and give people a glimpse inside another person's world. My own life is full of such wonder.

SOMETIMES THE NIGHT IS SMALL

Kofi Obeng was a college student at the University of North Dakota who, like me, had lived in both Africa and the U.S. and who became my friend. Kofi had grown up in Ghana. He came to our house for Thanksgiving and spent the day telling stories to my children, my niece, and my nephews.

"Put my stories into your books," he said.

I wasn't sure whether that would be possible, but I was intrigued by the story he told about Anansi, the West African trickster, and his description of a turtle muttering to himself: *Hand come. Hand go.*

The sensory details Kofi shared were full of power and charm and tugged me inside his childhood experience. I gave them to the little girl who was starting to tickle my mind.

> Abena closes her own eyes. In her mind she can see the huge moon hanging over her old home. An insect whistles. Fireflies flicker on-off-on-off and fried fish and nutmeg spice the air. Now she hears the storyteller's voice ringing through the village. "Anansi is a cheat!"

But I still needed to figure out exactly what shape the story would take and how those sensory details might fit. Eventually, my thoughts went back to what some would call my life's material. *Faraway Home* had let me offer a glimpse into the many children who are growing up thinking of the United States as home. Who stare at maps trying to imagine countries, mountains, deserts, valleys they've never seen but their parents have. Whose parents are homesick for faraway lands.

Kofi's stories gave me the chance to offer a peek at the children who arrive in the United States with only their flashlights, their stories, and their courage to try new things. Those children want to stay connected—as I did—with grandparents far away. *In the Small, Small Night* also gave me the chance to show, once again, that stories tie us to the things we love.

They gave me the chance to remember what it was like for me when I visited the United States as a child. What was I afraid of? (Nighttime in California came flooding back with the memory of how sure I was that a tarantula was climbing on my bed.) They gave me the chance to remember what it was like to tell stories to my younger siblings.

Illustration by Rachel Isadora from *In the Small, Small Night*. Credit: Illustrations copyright © 2005 by Rachel Isadora. Used by permission of HarperCollins Publishers.

I didn't know that by the time the book was published, I would be a grandparent with my own faraway grandbaby.

WRITERS THINK ABOUT WRITING

Vivid Details

Good writers are treasure hunters for vivid, interesting details that will pull the reader inside the experience or inside the writer's thoughts.

One way to be a treasure hunter is to do research, and one way to do research is to interview people. Study the scene where Abena thinks about how storytelling is done in her village in Ghana. List the details that have to do with each of the five senses. Those are details I coaxed out of my friend Kofi by asking him questions.

Rhythm and Beat

Good writers listen to the rhythms of sentences and pay attention to how one sentence flows into and fits with the next.

Usually, repeating words or sentences is a recipe for boredom, but sometimes writers do it on purpose. When I retold Kofi's Anansi story, I wanted to capture his storytelling voice, including the repetition. Use *In the Small, Small Night* as a model and play with repetition to create a pleasing sound in a piece of writing.

More Books

Many of my books are picture books, early readers, or novels for readers in elementary grades. In an effort to help others become better acquainted with the many voices and faces of the African continent, I have collected stories of ordinary and some not-so-ordinary people who have a connection with Africa. That anthology is *Memories of Sun: Stories of Africa and America.*

I have also written fantasy, including *The Feverbird's Claw.* Here are the brief stories behind those books and some yet to come.

WRITING FOR TEENS—*MEMORIES OF SUN: STORIES OF AFRICA AND AMERICA*

Every person who is alive or has ever lived on this earth has amazing stories to tell. Students in my writing workshops have written things that have stuck with me my whole life.

Michael, a fifth grader, wrote that the most amazing thing he ever saw was a cow giving birth to a calf. Nicole, a sixth grader, wrote about seeing her uncle pick up a silver spoon from China and eat a ladybug. Both of those students—and others—amazed *me* and made me see a few of the interesting things that go on right under our noses in this world. It's an important and wise and strong thing to take time to tell and listen to each other's stories.

I grew up in Ethiopia and by now have seen many parts of that country and of the continent of Africa. Sometimes I think that to most people in the United States, the whole huge continent of Africa is practically invisible. In 1997, I started my own journey of getting to know more of the African continent, myself. Over the next decade, I visited and spoke in public and private schools in Ethiopia, Uganda, Kenya, and Nigeria. I gave presentations and had conversations with teachers in Botswana, Senegal, Ghana, and South Africa. As I breathed in the hot, wet, thick air of Nigeria and watched traditional dances at one of the schools, I thought again about the way people in the United States sometimes ask me, "Do you know the African language?" But Nigeria alone has more than 200 languages.

Africa is a complicated swirl of languages, cultures, clothing, foods, geography, and customs. The North American continent, with all of its complexity, would fit in just one corner of Africa. I began to wonder if

Jane *(right)* and Angela Johnson at a writing retreat

Jane *(left)* in Uganda with Monica Arac de Nyeko

there was any way that writing could help teachers and librarians who wanted to help their students understand that Africa is not a country but a giant, complex continent.

One answer turned out to be a collection of short stories that I edited called *Memories of Sun: Stories of Africa and America.* My goal was to include stories by writers living in both Africa and America, stories that would appeal to middle-school readers about young people their age, stories both funny and sad, and stories from North, South, East, and West Africa. The stories collected in that book represent many facets of the African experience. One of my stories is included in the anthology: "Flim Flam." The other stories were written by various writers who had a connection to modern-day Africa, including Monica Arac de Nyeko and Angela Johnson.

THE FEVERBIRD'S CLAW—A FANTASY TAKES SHAPE

My love of fantasy started early. Whether I was shivering as I listened to a recording of *Peter and the Wolf,* reading fairy tale collections and weeping over the little mermaid when she turned to sea form, or staring at the animal on Agip gas station signs all over Addis Ababa, I loved the sensation of being transported to someplace eerie and fascinating.

In high school, I discovered *The Lord of the Rings* and sank into J.R.R. Tolkien's vivid world of hobbits and elves, wizards and orcs, with their histories and languages and old fights and new quests. Later, when I taught third and fourth graders at Carbondale New School, we curled in the reading corner and I read *Watership Down*—a long novel by Richard Adams about rabbits on a quest to find a new warren. When my students and I got to the end, we decided we liked it so much that we went back to the beginning and read it again.

So it wasn't too terribly astonishing that one day I decided I would write a fantasy novel. When I lived in Trinidad, Colorado, on a branch of

Cover art from *The Feverbird's Claw*, Copyright © 2004 by Don Seegmiller. Used by permission of HarperCollins Publisher.

the Santa Fe Trail, I read a lot of Southwest history, and I found myself fascinated by true stories of people such as Cynthia Ann Parker, captured by Comanches, who never adjusted to life back among her birth folks. Out of some back room of my mind, an idea swam up. I would write about a girl growing up sheltered and protected in a barricaded city, kidnapped by a roving band, determined to get home, finally managing—only to discover that she didn't belong there any more.

With the confidence of someone who hadn't yet experienced deep revision, I plunged. The draft was fun and it came pouring out. No doubt I would have shelved it right then and there if I'd known it would take thirteen years to finally become *The Feverbird's Claw*.

A PIRATE NOVEL IN THE MAKING

After *The Feverbird's Claw* was published, I wasn't sure I would ever write another fantasy novel, but that's before I spent a year or two—off and on—hanging around my brother. People are often curious to know what it's like to collaborate on a book. For me, collaboration has to start with someone I get along with really well, someone who knows how to laugh and makes me laugh, someone who loves to read as much as I do. My brother is one of those people.

By 2004, we were doing some presentations together—in states as diverse as Oregon, Washington, Texas, New Jersey, and Michigan. Christopher, an EEL teacher, was the one (when we sat with young readers at meet-the-authors lunches) to ask, "What books do you love?" The answers made us think about what we were writing.

After *Water Hole Waiting* was published, we'd written several more picture books together, books that so far haven't been published. The idea that had led us to *Water Hole Waiting* was a desire to write about rainy season and dry season. We tried that. Another time, since we both love playing music, we tried a picture book about a family of musicians. Christopher got more and more hooked. He decided to take a day off from teaching every week for his own writing and author presentations.

One day, we were walking near my house in Kansas. Christopher looked up at two rows of spooky trees that crossed arms over our heads and said, "Would you ever want to write about pirates?"

To tell the truth, up until that point, pirates had never showed up in my idea books, and I doubt they ever would have.

Christopher with his cat

"Remember the song we used to sing?" he asked. "The one about Henry Martin? It has plot, right? It might be fun to turn into a book."

"Huh," I said. "Henry Martin. We should at least look up the words to the song."

We quickly discovered that the ballad had been sung in the 1700s and maybe even earlier. Lots of different versions existed, including the one we used to sing.

> "There were three brothers in merry Scotland,
> In merry Scotland there were three,
> And they did cast lots which of them should go,
> should go, should go,
> And turn robber all on the salt sea.
> The lot it fell first upon Henry Martin,
> The youngest of all three;
> That he should turn robber all on the salt sea,
> Salt sea, salt sea.
> For to maintain his two brothers and he."

That ballad turned out to be the start of my first adventure in writing a novel with another person. Christopher and I began by talking a little bit about the characters. Something had to drive Henry Martin to sea. (It's almost always a productive question to ask: What does my main character want?) What would he find there? Who would his companions be?

Perhaps because we are both cat lovers, we seized onto one of the answers that came popping into our conversation: a talking cat.

By the end of our brainstorming conversation, I had some good ideas for the first chapter. We agreed that I'd write it and send it to him without telling him anything about where I thought the story was going. He'd write the second chapter and send it back. I'd write the third.

Easy.

It didn't quite work that way. Even though we both thought we were open to (and even excited by) the idea of having someone else take the story and possibly run in another direction than the one we'd had in mind, we quickly realized it was frustrating to waltz down a certain path only to have our writing partner yank the story in a completely different direction. Fortunately, we did quite a bit of speaking together during that year, and we ended up taking many long walks—in Boise, Idaho; in Northville, Michigan; in Portland, Oregon; in Washington, D.C.; in Atlantic City, New Jersey; and other places—hammering out details.

We asked each other and ourselves questions. Where were Mother and Father? What drove the bad guys to behave as they did? How, exactly, did communication work between humans and animals? We sometimes found ourselves gasping with laughter, wondering how our conversations would sound to someone overhearing them as we earnestly discussed octopus motivation or the subtle differences between ogres and tolgars or whether the third brother should be able to turn into any animal he wanted at any time—or were there limits on the magic?

As the chapters piled up, we kept pulling details from the sea. Crabs turned into guards. Seagulls became the ogre's spies. We sent ships crashing into high waves and scraping along reefs and drifting into misty coves where shrouded islands waited and mysteries lurked. We kept reading about the ocean, visiting the ocean, and making each other laugh.

The chapters we wrote made us laugh, too, and they made our agent laugh. Someday, we hope, someone will turn those chapters into a book that will make readers laugh. But even if that never happens, I'll always be glad for the fun of making up worlds and for the joy of hard work as I dig deep for events and characters to put in them.

PART III

Going Beyond the Writing

Libraries and Books in Ethiopia

Writing books helps to give voice to the many stories in the world. These books must then find readers. But as I saw in my childhood, many children in Ethiopia do not have access to books—now, thanks to the dream of one Ethiopian man, some of those young people are able to hold a book in their hands.

AFRICAN CONNECTIONS TODAY

This part of my story starts with visits to Nigeria, Uganda, Botswana, Kenya, and Senegal, where teachers and parents and even radio interviewers asked me, "How can we develop a reading culture in this country?" and "How can we start writing down the stories that are getting lost because children no longer sit at the feet of the elders?"

Those questions startled me and made me think about how my own mother and father became readers. I began to wonder how a reading

Jane signing books in Uganda

culture blossomed in the United States. I began to talk about how libraries are a treasure—and so are publishers and teachers and parents who are excited to share books with young readers.

In 2001, sixteen members of my family traveled back to Ethiopia together, and some of us even climbed a cliff to visit Maji. Who would have imagined that I would see the path to the bat cave and the

Jane with school staff and parents in Nigeria

waterfalls and even the water babies again? That two of my children, Jonathan and Rebekah, would go along?

Christmas Eve found us in Lalibela, singing a Christmas carol as we sat with Orthodox priests, who then blessed us with a holy song of their own. We sang again around the campfire at Maji.

It was a hallelujah kind of time, except for my daughter, who was struck by some kind of stomach ailment. She was still sick when the time came to struggle our way back down to the airport where the small Ethiopian Airlines airplane was going to whisk us back to Addis Ababa.

At the end of the trip, Jonathan, Rebekah, and I said our goodbyes to the others. I assumed it might be the last time I spent time in Ethiopia. I also thought it would no doubt be the only time my children visited Ethiopia.

Meanwhile, these African journeys found their way into my school presentations. Pictures were put into my presentations and on my Web site. And I talked about my journeys with students in the United States. In one school, a second-grade girl turned to an American-Ethiopian boy sitting next to her and asked, "Is that where you were born?"

He nodded his head shyly.

"Wow," she said. "You're lucky."

But from time to time, children would ask me a hard question. "Do kids in Ethiopia read your books?" I tried to explain that students in international schools could check my books out of the school library. But millions of young readers in Ethiopia didn't have any libraries or any books in their schools.

Maji today

"Can children in Ethiopia even read?" students and teachers asked me.

Reading, I said, was still taught by teachers who pointed to Amharic or Tigrinya or Oromo letters on a chart. And classrooms might hold up to 180 students who got to go to school for only half of the day. Although there were some bookstores, there were only a few black-and-white books available for children in any of the Ethiopian languages.

That was the way it had been all my life. That was the way I thought it would be for the rest of my life.

Student in international school looking at *Fire on the Mountain*

PLANTING READING SEEDS

One year, I got an e-mail from someone who cared a lot about those realities. His name was Yohannes Gebregeorgis, and he explained that he had fled from Ethiopia during the hard years of war and became a political refugee in the United States. He'd earned his college degree in Texas and then a master's of library science degree in New York state. Now he was a children's librarian at the San Francisco Public Library.

He told me he had never held a book in his hands outside of school until he was nineteen years old. When he read it, he discovered that books change lives. He also said, "We have to find a way to get books into the hands of Ethiopian children."

Yes, I thought. *But what can two people do?*

It took years, but I slowly came to believe we could find the support we needed. In Washington, D.C., an adoptive mom with two Ethiopian daughters collected some of Yohannes's ideas. Readers at the First Presbyterian Church in Grand Forks, North Dakota, read what she had collected and written down. One of them said, "I think we could do a piece of this."

The piece we chose was raising money and figuring out how to publish the first full-color children's picture book in both English and Amharic. Yohannes wrote down what he calls the favorite story told to children during his childhood in Ethiopia. He found an Ethiopian illustrator to do the pictures.

Children at the First Presbyterian Church did a read-a-thon. Other people gave us money and some good ideas. I asked for a volunteer on the Society

Cover art for *Silly Mammo: An Ethiopian Tale.* Credit: *Silly Mammo: An Ethiopian Tale*—Cover art by Bogale Belachew for *Silly Mammo: An Ethiopian Tale* by Gebregeorgis Yohannes. Illustration copyright © 2002 by Bogale Belachew. Used by permission of the Ethiopian Children's Book and Educational Foundation.

of Children's Book Writers announcement list, and children's book illustrator Janie Bynum stepped forward to design the book and oversee the printing.

When we held those books in our hands we thought we'd done something amazing, and our minds turned toward how to ship copies to Ethiopia. But Yohannes had different ideas. Enthused by such support for his dreams, he quit his job in California and moved back to Ethiopia. Six months later, he started the first free library for children in Addis Ababa, a city of five million people.

In April 2003, I cut the ribbon at the opening of Shola Children's Library. I asked Yohannes, "How do you plan to get the word out?" Clearly, I'd underestimated the hunger for education and a safe place where children felt welcomed. Without any advertising or publicity effort, the staff recorded 40,000 visits in the first year and 60,000 a year for the next two.

Today, a small but growing group of volunteers works to raise money to support Ethiopia Reads. Yohannes has started three rural libraries near where he grew up. (One is a mobile library with a cart full of books pulled by a donkey.) The next project will be simple reading rooms in schools that have never had libraries—and more children's books written in local languages for children to read and enjoy.

FULL CIRCLE

Rebekah *(left)* and Erin on their way

In 2004, two of my children—Rebekah and Jonathan—and my brother's daughter Erin went to Ethiopia to live in a poor neighborhood and volunteer at the Shola Children's Library. I was incredibly pleased and proud of them.

Erin and Rebekah lived in Ethiopia for five months, reading to children at the library, helping to get the word out to other Americans in the city of Addis Ababa, and trying to figure out how Ethiopia Reads could better do its work. Although they had hoped to stay longer, they found that homesickness kept nibbling at their resolve. Finally, Rebekah told me, "Mom, I think I can help more by coming back to the U.S. and designing a Web site for the project." That's what she did.

But Jonathan, as a young man, felt comfortable exploring the country. He wrote about his adventures on the bouncy old buses and hiking in the Simien Mountains. His departure date came and went several times, and he kept extending his ticket.

Eventually, we discovered one of the important reasons why. He was becoming close friends with the young woman who was the bookkeeper at the reading center. Friendship developed into something more and they married. That's how I came to have a granddaughter born in Ethiopia, the country where I moved as a two-year-old.

Jonathan with his daughter

Jane's daughter-in-law and grandbaby

I like showing off my pictures as much as any grandma does. In school visits these days, I tell the story of how I came to be a reader and writer, and then the story of how books changed Yohannes's life, and then the story about how Jonathan went to Ethiopia and married Hiwot. I put up a picture of Ellemae Enku. "Who do you think this is?" I ask. "If this is my son's little girl, what does that make her to me?

In Holland, a girl waved her hand, and I waited for her to say, "Your grandbaby." Instead, she gave me a great big smile and said, "Special."

Now that Jonathan and Hiwot are in the United States for college,

Enku getting a hug from her grandma *(me)*

Enku reading with her grandpa

Ellemae Enku is already a child of two continents. I don't know where she'll go to school. I don't know if she'll have a charmed life or one full of sorrow. I do know she will have stories to hang onto. And hopefully so will all of Ethiopia's children.

FOR MORE INFORMATION

If you wish to learn more about my trips to Ethiopia or to read more about the stories behind any of my books, please visit my Web site at http://www.janekurtz.com. On that Web site is a contact page; if you would like to e-mail me you can get my contact information there. I enjoy hearing from all types of readers.

If you would like to go beyond your own library borders and help children in Ethiopia to have books and libraries, visit the Ethiopia Reads Web site at http://ethiopiareads.org. You will find ordering information there for *Saba: Under the Hyena's Foot,* thanks to an American Girl Company donation of books to Ethiopia Reads. In a few years, I believe this world will have a whole new group of readers.

Photo Credits

All photos/graphics in this book were taken from the Kurtz/Goering family album or from Jane Kurtz's professional archives, except for the following photographs/graphics.

CHAPTER 3

Bicycle Madness—Book cover art illustrated by Beth Peck from *Bicycle Madness*. Illustrations © 2003 by Beth Peck. Reprinted by permission of Henry Holt and Company, LLC.

Do Kangaroos Wear Seat Belts?—Book cover art by Jane Manning from *Do Kangaroos Wear Seat Belts?* © 2005 by Jane Manning. Reprinted by permission of Dutton Children's Books.

Faraway Home—Illustrations from *Faraway Home* written by Jane Kurtz. Illustrations copyright © 2000 by E.B. Lewis. Reprinted by permission of Harcourt, Inc.

The Feverbird's Claw—Book cover art for *The Feverbird's Claw* © 2004 by Don Seegmiller. Used by permission of HarperCollins Publishers.

Fire on the Mountain—Book cover art reprinted with the permission of Simon & Schuster Books for Young Readers, an imprint of Simon & Schuster Children's Publishing Division from *Fire on the Mountain* by Jane Kurtz, illustrated by E.B. Lewis. Illustrations copyright © 1994 by E.B. Lewis.

I'm Sorry, Almira Ann—Book cover and interior art by Susan Havice from *I'm Sorry, Almira Ann*. Illustrations © 1999 by Susan Havice. Reprinted by permission of Henry Holt and Company, LLC.

In the Small, Small Night—Book cover art illustration copyright © 2005 by Rachel Isadora. Used by permission of HarperCollins Publishers.

Johnny Appleseed—Book cover art reprinted with the permission of Aladdin Paperbacks, an imprint of Simon & Schuster Children's Publishing Division from *Johnny Appleseed* by Jane Kurtz, illustrated by Mary Haverfield. Illustrations copyright © 2004 by Mary Haverfield.

Jakarta Missing—Book cover art for *Jakarta Missing*. Used by permission of HarperCollins Publishers.

Memories of Sun: Stories of Africa and America—Book cover art for *Memories of Sun: Stories of Africa and America*. Used by permission of HarperCollins Publishers.

Mister Bones: Dinosaur Hunter—Book cover art reprinted with the permission of Aladdin Paperbacks, an imprint of Simon & Schuster Children's Publishing Division from *Mister Bones: Dinosaur Hunter* by Jane Kurtz, illustrated by Mary Haverfield. Illustrations copyright © 2004 by Mary Haverfield.

Only a Pigeon—Book cover art reprinted with the permission of Simon & Schuster Books for Young Readers, an imprint of Simon & Schuster Children's Publishing Division from Jane Kurtz's *Only a Pigeon*, illustrated by E.B. Lewis. Illustrations copyright © 1997 by E.B. Lewis.

Pulling the Lion's Tail—Book cover art reprinted with permission of Ethiopian Children's Book and Educational Foundation, from Jane Kurtz's *Pulling the Lion's Tail*, illustrated by Eshetu Tiruneh. Illustrations copyright © 2006 by EBCEF.

Rain Romp: Stomping Away a Grouchy Day—Book cover art illustrations copyright © 2002 by Dyanna Wolcott. Used by permission of HarperCollins Publishers.

River Friendly, River Wild—Book cover art reprinted with the permission of Simon & Schuster Books for Young Readers, an imprint of Simon & Schuster Children's Publishing Division from *River Friendly, River Wild* by Jane Kurtz, illustrated by Neil Brennan. Illustrations copyright © 2000 by Neil Brennan.

Saba: Under the Hyena's Foot—Book cover art reprinted with permission of Pleasant Company Publications/American Girl.

The Storyteller's Beads—Book cover illustration from *The Storyteller's Beads* by Jane Kurtz copyright © 1998 by James Ransome. Reproduced by permission of Harcourt, Inc.

Trouble—Book cover illustration from *Trouble* by Jane Kurtz. Illustrations copyright © 1997 by Durga Bernhard. Reprinted by permission of Harcourt, Inc.

Water Hole Waiting—Book cover art for *Water Hole Waiting* copyright © 2002 by Lee Christiansen. Used by permission of HarperCollins Publishers.

CHAPTER 12

Only a Pigeon—Illustration of boy feeding a pigeon, for *Only a Pigeon*, reprinted with the permission of Simon & Schuster Books for Young Readers, an imprint of Simon & Schuster Children's Publishing Division from Jane Kurtz's *Only a Pigeon*, illustrated by E.B. Lewis. Illustrations copyright © 1997 by E.B. Lewis.

CHAPTER 15

Bicycle Madness—Illustration of Frances Willard on a bicycle by Beth Peck from *Bicycle Madness*. Illustrations © 2003 by Beth Peck. Reprinted by permission of Henry Holt and Company, LLC.

CHAPTER 16

In the Small, Small Night—Illustration of sister and brother from *In the Small, Small Night*. Illustration copyright © 2005 by Rachel Isadora. Used by permission of HarperCollins Publishers.

The Feverbird's Claw—Copyright © 2004 by Don Seegmiller. Used by permission of HarperCollins Publisher.

CHAPTER 18

Silly Mammo: An Ethiopian Tale—Cover art by Bogale Belachew for *Silly Mammo: An Ethiopian Tale* by Gebregeorgis Yohannes. Illustration copyright © 2002 by Bogale Belachew. Used by permission of the Ethiopian Children's Book and Educational Foundation.

Index

About the Author

JANE KURTZ has authored more than 22 books for early readers, nonfiction books, professional books for teachers, picture books, and novels that draw on her own childhood memories of growing up in Ethiopia, on living through the Red River flood of 1997, on her great gradmother's adventures traveling the Oregon Trail, and on the minor crises of her children's lives—from a friendship gone sour to the grouchiness of a rainy day. She currently lives (and writes) in Hesston, Kansas and maintains a website at www.janekurtz.com.